*Let's Talk* is certainly a light in these dark times. In a time when the world looks bleaker than ever, Rios encourages his readers to... focus on what matters most—spending time with family and friends, being thankful for the things you do have, and unwinding with a glass of wine. Highly recommended, *Let's Talk* is a fun, amusing, quick guide to the ways Rios has discovered that help him live a better life.

**—Rachel Song**, Writer and editor, ★★★★★

Buoyant, enlightening, inspiring, positive—and very useful! This book is so full of healthy, helpful energy that it just soars!

**—Grady Harp,** Amazon Hall of Fame Top 50 Reviewer, ★★★★★

Whatever your age or situation, you'll have a wonderful, enlightening time reading or listening to Art Rios, counselor extraordinaire. Highly recommended!

**—John Kelly,** Detroit Free Press, ★★★★★

The power of Art Rios' positivity shines through in this life-changing book. Highly recommended! An enlightening and inspirational self-help book.

**—Susan Keefe,** Midwest Book Review, ★★★★★

**BOOK 1**

# Let's Talk

## ...ABOUT MAKING YOUR LIFE EXCITING, EASIER, AND EXCEPTIONAL

# ART RIOS

ST. PETERSBURG
FLORIDA

Copyright © 2020 by Arturo R. Rios
Rios Talks Inc.
2929 Fifth Avenue North
St. Petersburg, Florida 33713
www.RiosTalks.com

All rights reserved.
No part of this book may be reproduced by any mechanical, photographic,
electronic, or any other process whatsoever, or in the form of a phonographic or audio recording
of any kind; nor may it be stored in a retrieval system, transmitted, or otherwise be copied for public
or private use—other than for "fair use" as a brief quotations embodied in articles and reviews—
without the prior written consent of the author.

The author of this book does not dispense medical advice or prescribe the
use of any technique herein as a form of treatment for physical, emotional, or
medical problems without the advice of a physician, either directly or indirectly.
The intent of the author is only to offer information of a general nature to help
you in your quest for emotional and spiritual well-being. In the event you
use any of the information in this book yourself, which is your right, the author
assumes no responsibility for your actions.

Published by Rios Talks, Inc.

Publisher's Cataloging-In-Publication Data
(Prepared by The Donohue Group, Inc.)

Names: Rios, Arturo R., author.
Title: Let's talk. Book 1 : ... about making your life exciting, easier, and exceptional / Art Rios.
Other Titles: About making your life exciting, easier, and excep-tional
Description: St. Petersburg, Florida : Rios Talks, [2020]
Identifiers: ISBN 9781735459905 | ISBN 9781735459912 (ebook)
Subjects: LCSH: Conduct of life. | Quality of life. | Happiness.
Classification: LCC BF637.C5 R56 2020 (print)
LCC BF637.C5 (ebook)
DDC 158.1—dc23

Cover and interior design by Dunn+Associates, www.Dunn-Design.com

Print Book: 978-1-7354599-0-5
Ebook: 978-1-7354599-1-2
Audio Book: 978-1-7354599-2-9

First Printing, 2020
Printed in the United States of America

In appreciation for buying my book . . .

# A 100% FREE Gift
# from Me to You . . .

The
*LET'S TALK*

Book One:

Quotes & Takeaways Booklet

To download go to: RiosTalks.com/free

Thank you and enjoy the book!

To God, for filling my life with purpose

To my daughters, for filling my life with joy

To my father, for filling my life with righteousness

To my mother, for filling my life with curiosity

To my sister, for filling my life with memories

To my wife, for filling my life!

*Talking to people is*

*the most educational thing*

*I know.*

—MARTY RUBIN

# Contents

# Let's Talk

**"Who is this 'Art Rios'?** Why listen to this bozo?" I can hear you asking yourself these questions. Let's talk.

They're fair questions. I'd ask the same. And I'll answer them, but first, let me say—thank you for reading this book. *Let's Talk* is my dream to help people live exciting, easier, and exceptional lives now, not tomorrow. Yep, exactly what the subtitle says, that's the goal of *Let's Talk*. Our talks will be about finding simple ways to leave the rat race, make life easier, and enjoy life's pleasures. I hope you'll join me on this glorious quest, that you'll find it engaging and fun, and that we'll become great friends along the way.

Right, so back to the question—"Who is this 'Art Rios'?"

I'm a trial lawyer—no wait! Don't close the book! We are not all bad.

In this case, being a lawyer is a good thing, as it makes me a counselor of sorts. I have learned a lot in courtrooms. But I've learned even more in the courtroom of life, where I've gained insight into human behavior. I've learned how people think and behave, in both good and bad times.

So, I'm a student of humanity. I cherish people. I love to chat with everyone. It is impossible for me not to like someone. I care about people, and I always have.

As a student of humanity, I wrote *Let's Talk* to share my observations on everyday life. And trust me, I'm a talker! The problem is that once I start talking, it's hard for me to stop. I love conversations. Although modern technology is fantastic, it has eroded dialogue. Actual face-to-face jibber jabber. Shooting the breeze. Running the mouth. Chewing the fat. Forget texting, forget messaging, forget social media and using some cartoon smiley face thingy to indicate some kind of something. I'm an advocate and, if I dare say so myself, a connoisseur, of good old-fashioned gab.

For example, when my daughters, Maria and Alondra, were younger, they would text one another, right across the table, when they could have simply talked. What the heck? *Let's Talk* is about reviving genuine conversations. Along the way, we can become friends and talk about ways to improve our lives and exchange tips on things we do that already bring us enjoyment and satisfaction. Which brings us to the topic, the BIG ISSUE, at hand . . .

When, where, why, and how did life stop being exciting and straightforward? The rat race—for most of us, it's like we're always in it. And not just at work. I'm talking on breaks at work, going to and from work, in the mornings before work and in the evenings after work, on the weekends, vacations—so much stress, tension, and worry all the time. Really? Why? And for what?

What I propose is that—within reason—we can have some fun and commit a few harmless misdeeds. And we can do so without going overboard and with moderation. Through *Let's Talk*, I want to be the guy you have the proverbial drink with to talk about the good life. Let the talks be a way for you to unwind and relax. To take a load off.

And what do I have to say? Our talks will be about anything and everything. From happy hour to self-realization. From pursuing pleasures to decluttering your life. We will even talk about sex and other "mature" topics, but always with the utmost dignity. I will never shock or embarrass you. I promise to be the consummate gentleman. *Let's Talk* exemplifies class and elegance. Nonetheless, there are classy and elegant ways to be naughty!

If you've heard of TED Talks, then you can consider *Let's Talk* the lite version. The fun version. The cool version. No heavy lifting. No walking through hot coals or jumping out of a plane. Unless you want to. You don't have to overthink our talks. You don't have to take notes, make outlines, or draw schematics. Simply relax and enjoy.

Let's not make this complicated. My aim is for you to ponder each talk and then say to yourself, "That makes sense," or you might say, "Art is full of crap." I'm cool with that. This is not dogma. It's straight talk about modern times. The subjects will be both timeless and timely. The things people have been thinking about for ages. Yes, even before smartphones. *Let's Talk* is not existential philosophy. Just simple ways to unwind and enjoy life.

We have become imprisoned by technology and by our jobs. Sure, there's nothing wrong with being ambitious, responsible, and hard-working. But, I'd hate for anyone to die wishing they'd enjoyed life more and worked less. Your final thought should be, "Man, I had a friggin' blast. An amazing life. No regrets. It's been a great run. A crapload of fun."

*Let's Talk* is about making your life a crapload of fun. Exhilarating. Titillating. An all-out blast! Again, with moderation and prudence. Whether you're 18 or 80, it's never too late to make the most of your life. As the incomparable Ricky Martin said, "I don't want to dream any more, I want my life to be real!" My fellow Boricuan is right. You're never too old, or too young, to have an exciting, easier, and exceptional life. That's why I want you to do it now! As Ricky says, make your dream life real now. Our talks will get you there.

One more thing before getting started. I'm sure you noticed how I said that these talks are meant to be "conversations." As you know, conversations are not monologues. So, how can we make this into a conversation? That's where my website and email come in—RiosTalks.com and Art@RiosTalks.com. If something I say really rattles your cage—in a good way or bad—contact me. Let's discuss it. Perhaps you have another slant, another idea, a different take related to one of my talk topics? Please share. What about an issue I don't discuss that you're super fired up about? Contact me. Bring it. I'd love to chew the cud with you. And if you'd like even more, you can join the *Let's Talk* club. As a member, you'll have access to videos, podcasts, on-line courses, webinars, an exclusive Facebook Mastermind group, and new content (as much or as little as you prefer). The member's fee is minimal, and part of the proceeds go to different charities. In Talk #4, you'll find the list of charities the *Let's Talk* club supports. So please consider it, I'd love to have you join.

Without further ado, welcome to *Let's Talk*. Please stay tuned. There's so much to discuss and enjoy—and what better way to do it than with a trusted friend? What a ride it will be, making your life exciting, easier, exceptional, and filled with pleasures!

Until we talk again, stay happy and healthy, my friend.

# Pursuing Pleasures

*Pleasure's a sin,*
*and sometimes sin's a pleasure.*
—LORD BYRON

**Great sex.** Excellent wine. Superb delights. Exotic escapes. Indulgent pampering. Do I have your attention? Pursuing pleasures is what life is all about. You only live once, so have a blast while you're here. Let's talk.

As long as you pursue pleasure with moderation and discretion, and you don't hurt anyone, then by all means—live every day to the fullest. Modern society seems to frown on pleasure-seeking. I'd like to know why. A little excitement and hedonism go a long way. But society would rather see you in the rat race until you're 65 or 70, and then retire to live the "good life." Bull manure. You must make your life exciting and easier now, not tomorrow.

What if, at 65 or 70, you can't live the good life? What if you can't eat rich foods then? What if you can't drink the wine then? What if you can't travel then? What if the genitals aren't up to par then? What will have been the point of all the sacrifice? Zero. Zip. Zilch. So, pursue pleasures now, today.

But first, determine what gives you pleasure. What you find pleasurable others may find tedious, so let's talk about some options.

The big kahuna is sex. Making love is life's grandest pleasure. In the next book, we will delve into the art of love. But, for now, put it at the top of your to-do list.

Moving on, wine is wonderful. So is beer and rum! We'll chat much more about this in our talks on happy hour and the one wine lunch. Bottom line, raise a glass and raise it often. *Cin cin. Salud. Skål.* Cheers, my friend.

And what better way to enjoy wine than with delicious food? From hot dogs to stroganoff, it's all fantastic. As long as you watch the waistline, eat it up!

Travel also ranks right up there in the pleasure list. Discovering unknown places and learning new cultures, seeing unfamiliar sights, and making new friends. What are you waiting for? Pack your bag and go. There's an entire planet to explore. I jump on Expedia.com all the time, looking for great travel deals and new adventures to pursue.

Exotic cars. Sparkling jewels. New homes. Elegant clothing. Fancy electronics. There are so many things we can enjoy. So why not? Give yourself the pleasure of splurging on that toy you want. But, keep it simple and easy, something we'll discuss more in Talk #6. Also, why buy when you can rent? You can use the money you save to enjoy even more pleasures.

Rest and relaxation. Kicking back and not doing anything. That is a tremendous pleasure. Talk #5 is all about lazy Sundays. Anything that helps you chill and unwind is a pleasure worth pursuing.

Indulging in the finer things will define your life. And they don't have to be extravagant, as you'll learn in Talk #9. Let's start with the pleasure of having a happy home. Make your home a bastion of love, joy, caring, welcome, hospitality, and celebration. Nothing can warm your heart, and everyone else's, more than a happy home.

Why not mix pleasures? Sex and spirits. Wine and chocolate. Cookies and cream. Travel and family. Sun-bathing and music. Strolling and holding hands. TV and laughing. Parents and reminiscing. Siblings and Scotch. Friends and phone calls. Children and hugging. Rain and loafing. Romance and candlelight. Pizza and beer. Napping on fresh sheets. Parks and picnics. Movies and munchies. These are all solid combinations.

Pursuing pleasures should also extend to providing pleasures, to being charitable. Give of your time, talent, and treasure. If God blesses you with resources, be a blessing to others. Being generous is a soulful pleasure. Courtesy and kindness go hand in hand with generosity. Showing empathy, caring, and kindness to others is the hallmark of class. I pride myself on being a kind gentleman at all times, and doing so fills me with immense satisfaction and happiness. Remember, a kind word and warm smile cost nothing. So give them generously. We'll talk more about this in Talk #14.

Reading is an enormous pleasure. Learning. Thinking. Meditating. Anything that gets the grey matter going is pleasurable. There's also great merit to fun novels.

An organized and uncluttered home is a pleasure. Sometimes solitude can be pleasurable. I love petting my dogs. Gorging on ice cream on a lazy Sunday is great. And so is having a good hair day. Hot tubs are relaxing. The sound of children's laughter is sublime. Need I go on?

Having defined your pleasures, remember, moderation is in order. Don't pursue pleasures beyond your means, so the pleasure won't become pain. Prudence is the key to pleasure. You need to take care of business first. As publisher and author William Feather so aptly noted, "Business is always interfering with pleasure, but it makes other pleasures possible."

Then again, your work may give you pleasure. If you love what you do, it's not work. It all depends on your attitude. Make work fun, or as Jack Canfield put it, "If you love your work, if you enjoy it, you're already a success." This mentality will go a long way towards making your life easier.

I get up every morning eager to write, record, and communicate with you through the website. It's not work. It is an incredible pleasure. You make that possible, so thank you and God bless you for it.

There is a caveat to pursuing pleasures: never do so at the expense of others. Your pleasures should never harm others. Never hurt another person's feelings or dignity. As in all things, pursue your pleasures with class.

Finally, don't let others define your pleasures. You are the sole judge of your desires and their propriety. Don't let society sway you. Of course, don't be vulgar. Comport yourself. But don't act just to please others either, as we'll discuss in Talk #3.

To summarize, don't put off your pleasures. Pursue them now, but with prudence. If you can, do something pleasurable every day. Remember, as French playwright Molière said, "Heaven prohibits certain pleasures; but one can generally negotiate a compromise."

Until we talk again, stay happy and healthy, my friend.

**1**

## TAKEAWAYS

- As long as you pursue pleasure with moderation and discretion, and you don't hurt anyone, then by all means—live every day to the fullest.

- Anything that helps you chill and unwind is a pleasure worth pursuing.

- If God blesses you with resources, be a blessing to others. Being generous is a soulful pleasure.

# Happy Hour

*I feel sorry for people who don't drink.*
*When they wake up in the morning,*
*that's as good as they're going to feel all day.*
—FRANK SINATRA

**Bring back happy hour.** What happened to it? I'm not talking about the new happy hour—people getting drunk on cheap drinks. Let's talk.

This talk is about the classic happy hour, like in the '50s, when people had a few martinis before dinner to unwind. It was a grand thing. So let's make life exciting, easier, and exceptional now by bringing back happy hour!

Any conversation about happy hour needs to start with a discussion about drinking. Drinking is in my blood. My whole family drinks, albeit some relatives imbibe more than others. It's an ingrained pleasure we enjoy. However, just to be clear—I'm not espousing heavy drinking.

Alcoholism or over-drinking is destructive. Drinking behooves moderation. I make this clarification because

I'm not fond of people who demonize drinking. I once heard, "You don't need alcohol to have fun. You don't need running shoes to run, but it helps!" Having a drink or two helps you relax. There's nothing wrong with enjoying a few drinks. There's nothing wrong with doing pretty much anything if it's legal.

For God's sake, the Bible says drinking is okay. "Stop drinking only water, and use a little wine." That's straight out of the Bible, 1 Timothy 5:23. And Ecclesiastes 9:7 instructs, "Eat your food with gladness and drink your wine with a joyful heart, for God has already approved what you do." God approves and has no problem with you having a few glasses of wine.

So, to the anti-drinking crowd, chill out! If you don't drink, that's great. I have no problem with that, as long as you don't have a problem with my happy hour. Live and let live.

*Let's Talk* is about enjoying life. About pursuing indulgence and pleasure. Drinking is a grand pleasure life has to offer. If not, God would not have created wine or inspired its creation.

But, if you have a drinking problem, confront it immediately. Please see a doctor right away. There are remedies. You can learn to drink in moderation. And if you can't, I pray for your recovery. Please seek professional help. Visit www.alcohol.org for guidance. With that said, if you can drink with moderation, then happy hour it is.

Happy hour should take place after work, preferably at home. It should last—you guessed it—about an hour. You get home, kiss your significant other, your kids, if they're home, you freshen up, and get it on!

Dress nicely. You feel better when you do, and you want to feel great during happy hour. I'm not saying to put on a tux, although that might be cool. Wear shorts and a polo shirt if you want. For the ladies, wear something that makes you feel classy. No matter the attire, feel comfortable and elegant.

To me, happy hour is family sharing time. It's a time to laugh, a time for joy, a time to share the day's happenings. Two stiff drinks should do the trick. And I don't mean two buckets of Scotch, for the conniving ones out there. I'm proposing having a couple of cocktails or glasses of wine before dinner.

Going back to family, happy hour is for family. I even get the dogs involved. Not that I give them alcohol, for Pete's sake, but Sofi, Zara, and Lulu are around to partake in the festivities. And Maria and Alondra, our daughters, join in the conversation when they're home from school. Alondra does not drink much—she's a singer and protects her voice—but she talks profusely. A real motormouth. (Wonder where she got that from?) Maria is of age and joins in the imbibing. I'm telling you, it's in our blood!

I also think happy hour should be a weekday thing, not a weekend thing. Leave the socializing, meaning the bigger get-togethers, for the weekend. And on the weekend, why limit the extravaganza to one hour? Again, with moderation.

I keep emphasizing safe drinking because I despise drinking and driving. Friend, even if you have one drink, do not get behind the wheel. Don't even get on a bicycle. That's why I suggest happy hour be at home. If your happy hour is at a restaurant or bar, get an Uber. Do not drink and drive.

Back to happy hour mechanics. Monday through Thursday with family. You may skip a day now and then, it's just better more often than not. Leave the weekends for socializing with friends and other relatives, and then you can extend it past the hour.

My wife, Sharon, and I treat happy hour as a ritual. I'll wrap up work around five, and it's happy hour. Sharon will be ready. She's finished for the day, freshens up, and gets even more beautiful than she always is. I freshen up and may also change. As you know, elegance is part of the ritual.

We like to add variety to happy hour, so we vary our drinks. For example, yesterday we had Scotch. I know that tonight we're having martinis, as Sharon bought blue-cheese-stuffed olives. Again, a ritual. I'll take out the martini glasses because you gotta drink in the proper glass—and *voilà*—happy hour begins. Sharon likes to fix something to nibble on before dinner. Or we might make it drinks and tapas, no dinner.

Another part of the ritual is no phones. The television is also off. No news. No distractions. For Sharon and me, the rare and sole exception: sometimes we may watch a hilarious gossip show, *El Gordo y La Flaca*, that comes on Univision around that time. But generally, the TV is off. Instead, I have a playlist with relaxing music, mellow versions of '80s songs. The music is not loud because our conversation rules.

I also like to know the evening's menu. Sharon is an incredible cook. If you've seen my picture, you won't find that hard to believe. I try to pair our drinks with the menu, to get the taste buds prepped. Not that I am a gourmand or food snob. I'm talking about common-sense pairings, stuff you can learn on the internet in two minutes. For example: sushi and saké; pizza and Pinot; tacos and Tequila; steak and Scotch. Screw the rat race and live it up!

Happy hour can also be a time to make memories. For example, my niece, Myrna Victoria, who is 22, spent two weeks with us recently. We loved having her. She fell in love with the happy hour ritual. It was hilarious. She would text me around 4:45 pm to see if I was finishing work. She'd let me know she was ready for happy hour! So, include family. It makes happy hour extra enjoyable.

Quite often my parents join us for happy hour. I love it when they do. We always have such a great time. When my parents are together, which is always, it's happy hour. I have never seen two people love each other more.

Sometimes I'll have a "special guest" over for happy hour. Maybe a good friend or neighbor. Just last week, my great friend David came to the house to drop off some coffee he'd gotten for us. His visit was opportune: I was just finishing mixing rum and cokes when the doorbell rang. Yada yada yada—David left 90 minutes later. The next day he called me around six and said, "Hey, Art, guess what I'm doing? Happy hour!" So, I do it to get people into the ritual. I invite them to see what we do and spread the ritual around. I am a big proponent of spreading happiness.

At other times, if I have to meet with a business associate, I'll invite them over to the house. We'll have our meeting, and then I ask them to stay for happy hour. Again, as long as drinking and driving is not an issue. I've made good connections this way, not just in the business sense, but friendship-wise.

Having happy hour at a lounge or restaurant is also nice. But, I can't emphasize this enough, it's about having a few drinks to relax and decrease stress. Don't get impaired.

I say this because *Let's Talk* is about enjoying all the pleasures life has to offer. And you can't enjoy pleasure without all your senses chiming in to the experience. Remember, happy hour lasts an hour. Other pleasures will follow after, like a great dinner. Maybe even a little romance after dinner, if you know what I mean. So, don't dull your senses at happy hour.

I remember seeing a sign in a bar that said, "Alcohol may not solve your problems, but neither will water or milk." Well, that is very true. Having a drink or two takes the edge off. Happy hour is the perfect way to do so. You'll find inspiration, and sometimes even enlightenment, during happy hour. It's a time to make plans, to share dreams, to envision success, and to enjoy the fruits of your labor. Happy hour also helps get you through the tough times because it gives you a designated space to hash things out and put them in perspective. Conversely, you can use happy hour as a time not to hash things out, but to laugh and remember, which also gives good perspective.

I hope that you'll start celebrating happy hour today! Raise your glass to me tonight during happy hour. I promise I'll raise mine to you. With glasses raised, I'll leave you with a quote from one of history's most superlative drinkers, Sir Winston Churchill, who said, "I have taken more out of alcohol than alcohol has taken out of me." *Salud*. Cheers. *Skål*.

Until we talk again, stay happy and healthy, my friend.

## 2   TAKEAWAYS

- Having a drink or two helps you relax. There's nothing wrong with enjoying a few drinks.

- Happy hour lasts an hour. Other pleasures will follow after . . . so don't overindulge.

- You'll find inspiration and enlightenment during happy hour. It's a time to make plans, to share dreams, to envision success, and to enjoy the fruits of your labor.

# Be Yourself

*Be yourself.*
*Everybody else is taken.*
—OSCAR WILDE

**This talk is an important one.** A serious issue. Many of us have felt that we're not good enough, that other people are better, and that we'd like to be like them. The crux of the matter: that kind of thinking is misguided. As Mr. Wilde said, you must be yourself. Let's talk.

You are unique. There's no one else like you. Nobody can be better than you because nobody else is you. Nobody has your distinctive talents and traits.

We all have unique gifts. We're all here for a reason. God gives us abilities that align with His master plan. If you want to be religious about it, it is God's will. Or, you can be philosophical and say that we fit a universal plan.

What does being yourself even mean? I'll start by sharing something personal. When I was a teenager, I couldn't find myself, my voice, my persona. I'm not sure why. Maybe I wasn't looking. Instead, I admired certain people too much. My father, my grandfather Papote, and my Uncle Coco come to mind. Another was a professional golfer. And obviously, James Bond! To me, they were so excellent that I tried to live their lives. I imitated them to a fault. I'd act, talk, and even walk a bit like them. I don't know if that's psychotic, but I don't think so. Maybe everybody goes through a phase like this, to some degree.

But I took it a step further in that it lasted longer than it should have. It went on through my twenties. The tendency waned after I married Sharon and we had the girls.

Rational or not, it took me too long to realize that I'm a nifty person. We all are. I don't have a lot of regrets, but looking back, I may have missed out, for too many years, on living life through my own eyes. Instead, I lived through the eyes of others for much too long. And this issue knows no age limits.

When we're young, our determination is boundless. I felt that way, but wasted my time trying to live in someone else's skin. It passed, and the day came when I finally found myself and realized I wasn't inferior. I was me, and I was reborn.

I now realize that I have abilities that God gave me for a reason. We all do. We don't have to imitate anyone. There's nothing wrong with admiring people, just don't obsess over them.

This admiration may carry on into our older years. But thankfully, as we get older, we mature and grow wiser. Our responsibilities may thwart our flights of fancy. However, a graver danger can arise: that same wisdom and maturity may bind us to the rat race. So while we must embrace the advantages of aging, we mustn't leave behind the youthful bravado, hope, and curiosity essential to living an exciting, easier, and exceptional life.

Something else—everyone has faults. You may think another person has it all, that they have no cares in the world, but that's not the case. Other people may have problems you can't even imagine.

Being yourself is essential because we put off our dreams by thinking we're not enough, that we don't have what it takes, that what we're interested in isn't right and we ought to chase after something else. My friend, you have everything you need to fulfill your dreams. They're your dreams, and no one else's. Never give up on them.

To illustrate, I'm a big guy. I've got a little extra blubber on me. Not obese, but chunky. And I always have been. But I'm okay with my weight. It's part of who I am. It defines my uniqueness and my personality. I'm very healthy, my wife thinks I'm sexy, so all is well.

But my weight bothered me for a long time. I thought I had to be thin to do everything I wanted to do. You know, if I wanted to be happy, I had to be thinner. To find love, to give love, to be a good dad, to find success at my job, whatever it was, I assumed it could only happen if I weighed less. That was a colossal mistake, and I realized it thanks to Oprah Winfrey. She's battled with her weight also. But she finally accepted it and said, "The essence of who I am has nothing to do with what I look like."

Thanks to Ms. Winfrey, I know that the love I give, the gifts I offer, and my life's mission is not beholden to my looks. I hope she reads this, and if so, thank you, Ms. Winfrey. Your words are profound. They changed my life. When I heard them, I realized I couldn't curb my potential because I'm no dreamboat. I'm a big guy and I enjoy it, love handles and all!

I've lost weight in the past. I've been on yo-yo diets. Up and down. It's crazy. I've been thinner than I am now, and honestly, I didn't feel great. It didn't go with my personality. I have the character of a chubby guy. My credo—if you have to lose weight for medical reasons, do it. If not, screw it!

In full disclosure, I had bariatric surgery many years ago. I was obese, and it weighed on me (get the pun?!). So I had LAP-BAND surgery, and it's the best decision I've ever made. I lost close to a hundred pounds. Yep, I'm still chubby, but I feel amazing. My doctor tells me I'm in great shape. If I ever have to lose weight for medical reasons, I will. But for now, I'm great the way I am.

The big takeaway—I want you to realize that nothing can stop you from achieving your dreams. Well, almost nothing. You can by not accepting yourself. However, once you embrace your imperfect self and your particular dreams, then nothing can stop you from achieving them. Nothing. It's never too late. Colonel Sanders sold the first Kentucky Fried Chicken franchise when he was 62. He'd failed at many things before but never gave up on his dream. And today, you can buy his Original Recipe chicken anywhere in the world!

Another quick example—*Let's Talk* was an idea I had for many years. I started the project many times, but always put it off. Then I heard Oprah's words and realized I couldn't put it off anymore. God wanted me to do this.

So, don't put anything off because you don't feel equipped to do it. Be yourself, and do what your heart and soul are begging you to do. Or, as author and motivational speaker Jack Canfield said, "Don't censor your dreams or vision with practicalities and probabilities."

Still not convinced? Then write down all of your outstanding qualities, along with the bad ones. Take measure. What do you see? The good ones outweigh the bad, and if they don't, then you're being too harsh on yourself. If you're honest, the good will outweigh the bad. You are capable of fulfilling your exceptional destiny.

You're a great person. Being yourself is the best thing you can do. Don't be what others want you to be. Or how you assume others want you to be. Because if you do, you'll never be you.

I mean, don't act illegally or immorally (at least, not too much!). I'm sure the thought didn't even cross your mind. But don't meld into society's unexciting mold. Be yourself so that everyone, including you, can enjoy your God-given uniqueness.

You're not alone. Others had problems being themselves but overcame it. As John Wooden, the "Wizard of Westwood," urged, "You have to be what you are. Don't be somebody else. Be yourself at all times." When you think about it, it's tough to act like somebody else. It's not natural. Being yourself is easy because you don't have to act.

Rock-n-roller Henry Rollins felt, "One defines himself by reinvention. To not be like your parents. To not be like your friends. To be yourself. To cut yourself out of stone." Heed Henry's words, carve yourself into a masterpiece. Chisel out the bad, and hallmark the great masterpiece that is you.

Bruce Lee said, "Always be yourself, express yourself, have faith in yourself, do not go out and look for a successful personality and duplicate it." That's it! You must always be yourself and not duplicate anyone else.

Who you are is all you can, must, and should be. You're better than anybody else because you can't be anybody else. I'm not saying you're superior, but you are unique. Never aspire to be anyone else.

Have faith in yourself. Don't look for a successful personality to emulate. Don't copy people. Being yourself is where your strength lies. Your gifts and blessings are yours alone. God gave them to you for a reason.

When you embrace yourself and your particular gifts and blessings, you'll be happier for it. You'll live your own life. You'll relish pursuing pleasures because they'll be self-defined. You'll only go after the things you really want. You will enjoy an exciting, easier, and exceptional life.

Above all, by being yourself, you fulfill your destiny. It's your unique gifts, thoughts, and ideas that the world needs. No one else can give them to the world because they're yours. Be yourself and bask in the power derived from self-realization. As Steve Jobs said, "Your time is limited, so don't waste it living someone else's life."

Until we talk again, stay happy and healthy, my friend.

**3**

## TAKEAWAYS

- You are unique. Nobody can be better than you because nobody else is you.

- Once you embrace your imperfect self and your particular dreams, nothing can stop you from achieving them.

- Who you are is all you can, must, and should be. Never aspire to be anyone else.

# Gratitude

*If the only prayer you said was
thank you, that would be enough.*
—MEISTER ECKHART

**Because I consider gratitude** the most essential of all traits, our talk on gratitude, to me, is our most important. It's a discussion we must all have. So Eckhart is right, an all-encompassing prayer of thanks is all we'll ever need. Let's talk.

I start each day with a prayer of gratitude, a "thank you, God." I thank Him for my life. For my home. For my girls' well-being. For my wife. For all my family. And for the world. Starting your day with gratitude fills your heart and kick-starts your day.

During the day, whenever I close my eyes for a quick rest, I also make it a point to thank God. And I end my day with gratitude, a heartfelt thank you to the universe for the day's blessings.

You should also thank everyone who's had a hand in your success. Whatever you have accomplished, you haven't done it alone. I'm sure someone helped along the way, and they deserve your gratitude. As you shun the rat race, thank those who are facilitating your ability to do so.

Everybody loves to hear a heartfelt thank you. There's impressive power in saying thank you, as gratitude begets sincerity. When you acknowledge somebody, you disarm them. Positivity flows from thankfulness.

I thank people every day. I'm a grateful person. And don't think my life has always been peachy. I've had my difficulties, and I've had them big. But even when I was at my lowest, when I was facing considerable challenges, I was always grateful. I was still appreciative because I was alive, and I knew that my gratitude would get me through.

Many people only pray in bad times. But it's more important to be grateful when everything is going well. Remember, life is never perfect. Everyone has travails.

So, pray when things are good and bad. In the dreadful times, your gratitude will be your armor. Things may be tough, but you're in the fight.

Now, this may sound harsh, but ingrates lack heart. Gratitude warms your soul, but ingrates have no warmth.

That's a sad way to live. We all have something to be grateful for, and taking time to show gratitude is easy.

I did the math. There are 1,440 minutes in a day. It only takes a moment to stop, reflect, and be thankful for your blessings. Take a few minutes, out of the 1,440 you have every single day, to say that brief prayer of gratitude.

And while you're at it, don't forget to thank yourself! We often forget to thank ourselves for what we have accomplished. Your dedication and hard work provide for you and your loved ones. So thank yourself—pat yourself on the back. After all, it's your hard work that allows you to live an exciting and easier life. And it's your daily practice of gratitude that makes your life exceptional.

Also thank your significant other, your parents, and everyone who's helped shape your life for the better. The Ancient Roman statesman and philosopher Cicero said, "Gratitude is not only the greatest of virtues, but the parent of all others."

Gratitude is the foundation for all human virtues. Gratitude is the cornerstone of a person's character. Gratitude begets exceptionalism. Again, don't forget to show others appreciation. No matter their station in life, thank them for any service or kindness they may show you.

Gratitude also enhances you physically. Your smile and your eyes radiate warmth when you say thank you. I hope you will watch my videos at RiosTalks.com. You will see the sincerity behind my appreciation for your support because, thanks to you, my dreams are coming true.

If we have auras, gratitude makes them sparkle. Your spark will be a beacon that will attract others. Gratitude is a magnet for marvelous things. The unequaled Oprah Winfrey is grateful for all her blessings. It's because she's so thankful that her blessings keep mounting. And she deserves them. Ms. Winfrey radiates that aura. She said, "Be thankful for what you have, and you'll end up having more. If you concentrate on what you do not have, you will never ever have enough."

Think about it. How many people buy a car, and instead of enjoying it, almost immediately start dreaming about the next one, hoping it will be better? They don't enjoy what they have now, which is the moment to enjoy things the most.

So, be thankful for what you have, and don't worry about what you want. Be thankful for what you have today. Tomorrow will take care of itself. Nothing makes life easier than being content with what you have. And being grateful forges the way to contentedness. They go hand in hand.

Being a noble person starts with an innate sense of gratitude. When you're grateful, you become fearless. You don't fret over what may be lacking in your life or over what tomorrow may bring. A grateful person lives in the present, with peace and happiness. This is an exceptional way to live.

Gratitude fuels your karma and is a great practice to teach your children. Teach them to be thankful, to say thank you frequently, as gratitude is a precursor to humility. If you teach your children to live in gratitude, you empower them for happiness. They'll love and be loved by others. They'll live exceptional lives.

In conclusion, take a few of the 1,440 minutes in your day to say thank you. Wake up and fall asleep thanking God. The universe will reward you tenfold for your gratitude, and you will have peace.

And lest I forget, thank you again for supporting *Let's Talk*. I am forever in your debt, and I pray God will repay you for it. As a token of my gratitude, visit www. RiosTalks.com and download Talk #4: Gratitude course video for free.

As always, I leave you with a great quote. When Buddha pondered gratitude, he determined, "Let us rise up and be thankful, for if we didn't learn a lot today, at least we learned a little, and if we didn't learn a little, at least we didn't get sick, and if we got sick, at least we didn't die; so, let us all be thankful."

Until we talk again, stay happy and healthy, my friend.

## 4   TAKEAWAYS

- Start each day with a prayer of gratitude, a "thank you, God."

- Don't forget to thank yourself! We often forget to thank ourselves for what we have accomplished.

- Gratitude is the foundation for all human virtues. Gratitude is the cornerstone of a person's character and makes for an exceptional life.

# Lazy Sundays

*Sundays are for lounging around in your underwear,
out-sleeping hangovers, and avoiding mirrors.
Any energy unduly spent angers the Sunday Gods,
and, therefore, it's your moral duty to stay in bed,
wrap yourself up in 12 layers, and binge watch.*
—TOM PROCTOR

**Few pleasures surpass** or make life easier than lazy Sundays, especially if your Saturdays are wild! Admittedly, I'm breaking my own lazy Sunday rule because I'm working on this talk on a Sunday. But, Scout's honor, I rarely work on Sundays. Even now, my motivation for writing this chapter today is because I figure it'll be better if I write it in the proper lazy Sunday groove. Let's talk.

Mr. Proctor is right. Sundays are for lounging, for recuperating after Saturday, and for being lazy. I am not reinventing the wheel here. The concept of lazy Sundays has been around since the dawn of time. Even God rested on Sunday!

I read somewhere that on Sunday, you sleep until you're hungry and eat until you're sleepy. Isn't that a fantastic plan? It should put us in the right frame of mind. My Sundays are religiously lazy, no pun intended.

My angelic wife respects my lazy Sundays. She is quiet in the morning and prepares a brunch that is ready by the time I get up, which is usually around lunchtime. The aromas of her food preparation usually wake me up. She'll warm leftovers because we rarely cook on Sundays. And we don't like to go out on Sundays either.

So, wake up, have brunch, then maybe read a book or watch TV. At some point, take a nap! Do it outside, get some fresh air. I may also do a little earthing outside.

"What is earthing?" I hear you ask.

Earthing is planting your bare feet in the grass to discharge the electric buildup in your body. To ground yourself. It may sound hokey, but it can't hurt.

Another lazy Sunday activity may be a little "afternoon delight." If you don't know what that means, look it up. I don't mean to be untoward, but we're all adults here. Why not have some naughty fun on a lazy Sunday? However, that's as physical as I get on Sundays.

I want to chill out, eat great food, take naps, and binge watch or read. I record a few television shows during the week. I'm not a tremendous TV fan; I prefer to read.

But Sundays are perfect for catching up on the few shows I do like. Or to watch brilliant movies, which I love, as I am a suppressed actor.

One thing I dislike doing on Sundays is drinking. I'm saying this because I don't want you to think I'm an alcoholic. You know, I've already discussed, promoted really, happy hour, and we'll soon talk about the one wine lunch. So, take note, I'm no lush! I rarely drink on Sundays. I suppose that I want my liver to enjoy a lazy day as well! I drink a ton of water to flush out the old system. But, if your laziness includes opening a bottle of wine, go for it.

A topic that may hinder lazy Sundays—and, God, please do not smite me—is going to church. I know that sounds horrible, but hear me out. Those of you that are devout churchgoers, keep going. Start your lazy Sunday right after church, filled with the peace and joy that worshiping provides. I'm a frequent churchgoer and feel remorseful when I don't go. But as I pray incessantly, I hope the Big Guy will forgive my missing the occasional Sunday.

Get this: even showers are optional on Sundays. Talk about making life easier! I sometimes start my Sundays with a relaxing bath. But on some Sundays, I get up, wash my face, brush my teeth, and the laziness begins. Just like that.

Also, there's always the option of spending lazy Sundays in your pajamas. I have a lazy Sunday outfit. For me, it's my Ralph Lauren jammies. And no shoes! Then, donned in my Sunday armor, it's brunchtime. Followed by couch-potato time. Brilliant.

There is a rough part to Sunday: thinking about Monday. We all dread the thought of going back to the damn rat race after an exciting weekend. But, if you're lazy on Sunday, you won't fret about Monday. To the contrary, start planning your week on Sunday evening. Think ahead, but not too much. Bask in the upcoming opportunities, and be positive about the week to come. And don't just plan for work, plan for exciting and exceptional things to do that week. Also, think about steps you can take to make your life easier in the coming week.

Another lazy Sunday activity is meditation. Keep it simple. You don't have to sit in the lotus position, chanting mantras with incense fired up, unless you want to. Meditation clears the mind, and starting the week with a clear mind will put you ahead of the pack.

I'll wind this talk down as it is Sunday, and I need to be lazy. I hope that all your Sundays will be lazy from now on. Make it a ritual. Your mind, body, and soul will thank you for it.

As always, I leave you with a great quote, this one from animator and film director John Lasseter: "Sunday is all about being home with the family with no plans."

Until we talk again, stay happy and healthy, my friend.

## 5 TAKEAWAYS

- Few pleasures surpass or make life easier than lazy Sundays, especially if your Saturdays are wild!

- On Sunday, you sleep until you're hungry and eat until you're sleepy.

- If you're lazy on Sunday, you won't fret about Monday.

# KISSing

*Keep it simple, stupid!*
—UNITED STATES NAVY

**Can anything beat a kiss?** That big smooch you hope lasts forever. The kisses we saw in old movies, where kissing was as provocative as it got. Think Rhett Butler kissing Scarlett O'Hara, long and hard. You get the picture. Serious, hard-core kissing. Let's talk.

First off—get your mind out of the gutter! I will not be offering French kissing lessons here—jeez! KISSing, in this regard, is about keeping things simple. It's about decluttering, simplifying, and minimizing. But, I reserve the right to revisit the art of kissing in the future. This talk will be about letting go of the superfluous stuff we tend to accumulate. To love living with less.

As we live in a materialistic society, we are victims of the consumerism monster. Think about it—the whole model of capitalism depends on an ever-growing economy. For that to happen, we must always think we don't have enough stuff. Or we don't have the right stuff. So we want more, buy more, want more, buy more. Indefinitely. To assist us in the never-satiating cycle of wanting and buying, we've got advertising bombarding us at every turn, always selling us the idea that we don't have enough. That there's this other thing we "must have."

The good news—few things are "must-haves."

The weapon to slay the "must-have" monster is KISSing. It's living with bareness and simplicity. Having essential necessities and not accumulating unnecessary things. In short, not having a bunch of crap lying around.

The Swedes have fine-tuned this concept, which they call *lagom*. It means "just the right amount." In other words, moderation. Take the Swedish proverb, "*Lagom är bäst*," which literally means, "The right amount is best," and the more fun translation, "Enough is as good as a feast." *Lagom* is appropriateness, not lavishness. And, like *lagom*, KISSing is about getting rid of the clutter in your life. It is simplifying everything, deciding what's essential, and living with only that. It's about living *lagom*-style.

Please note: KISSing is not about deprivation or sacrifice. It is about "Keeping It Stupidly Simple." This is a crucial step in making life easier, so you can enjoy its pleasures. You define what is enough for yourself. Be honest with yourself. If you must keep certain things that you treasure or worked hard for, keep them. If you don't treasure them, get rid of them.

The bottom line, having less stuff is great. You will have fewer things to clean, maintain, fix, pay for, worry about, and obsess over. Best of all, the less you have, the more space and freedom you have. The more freedom you have, the easier life becomes. And the easier life becomes, the more pleasurable it can be.

Having less certainly eases your financial burdens: less debt, less expenses, and less headaches, but more money in the bank. And what do we do with that money? You guessed it, enjoy life more. More guilty pleasures. More time and resources for hedonistic pursuits. And more resources for spreading kindness.

Are you sold? Okay, then on to nuts-and-bolts time. Let's talk about how we can make life easier by ditching all the extra crap we have.

The starting point is philosophical and existential. You need to take stock of what is important to you. You need to make an inventory of what you have and then decide whether it is something you need. It's a hard choice: want versus need.

But before we proceed, once again, I am not suggesting you ditch everything and live like an ascetic. Differentiate between your needs and wants. There are things of sentimental value that you may want to keep. Here is a way to resolve this: take a picture of the item with your smartphone. Will seeing the image of the article have as much meaning as keeping it? If so, keep the picture and ditch the thing. Problem solved. Memory saved forever. Boom.

Buying stuff is like an orgasm. But not as good! The satisfaction is very short-lived. As in decisions of the flesh, do a risk-versus-reward analysis. Honestly, sex beats abstinence. But if it's about buying something you don't need, then the decision is easier. But to clarify, it's completely okay to want some things and to buy some of those things, just don't want and buy everything. Pleasure includes owning a few select quality items. I certainly own nice things. What I'm warning against is buying just for the sake of buying—to satisfy an urge to buy likely spurred subliminally by the advertising monster.

It comes down to whether the item is of daily importance or a capricious want. Again, if it's a soulful want, go for it! But remember, your possessions don't define you. The worth of your things doesn't define your worth.

What you give, not what you buy, defines you—giving as a person, a parent, a spouse, a sibling, a son or daughter, a neighbor, a community member. Your compassion and the love you exude—that's what defines you. Your car does not. Sadly, many people still judge others by their possessions, not their personalities. By their castle, instead of their character.

Yet history has shown us that the most influential figures had next to nothing. Jesus, Mother Teresa, Gandhi, and Buddha jump to mind. They never had to worry about material goods because they shunned them. So, like the masters, we need to let things go. We must get rid of our superfluous possessions. But remember to allow yourselves some treasures. Even Jesus had a Holy Grail!

After you've taken stock of what's important to you, take stock of the physical items in your life. Look around your home and office. Start questioning the necessity of everything you see. If you were to donate, sell, or give away your extra things, might they be put to better use by others? Are the things you don't need needed by others? How many people would you help, how many burdens may you ease, by getting rid of your extra stuff? A lot.

Do you need 12 pairs of pants? Thirty shirts? Three cars? Six TVs? Two houses? You don't. But you don't have to throw it all away either. Sell it, take it to a pawnshop, auction it online, or donate it to a charity and get a tax deduction for your generosity. Everybody wins this way.

Granted, the thought of KISSing may daunt you, so if you own a load of crap, start little by little. Start with a drawer. Then finish the room. Go on to the next room, etc. Don't do it all at once. You didn't buy everything you own in a day. So take your time. Like me, you may look back on the process and realize that it was liberating and enjoyable.

You can't buy happiness. Getting a fancy new car can be great, but the joy is fleeting. Again, if getting the lux car is a life goal, go for it. You'll find Talk #9 is dedicated to going for the extra and, maybe, the once-in-a-lifetime extravagant purchase. But, my point now is that once accomplished, move on, and don't start thinking about getting a better one. I have owned and enjoyed great cars. But looking back, I wish I had saved the money instead. Heck, I'm thinking of getting rid of my car and Ubering everywhere. Life would be so much easier. No more car payments, insurance payments, gas costs, and repair costs. And I'd never have to look for parking! But that's KISSing for me, and how I KISS may not be the way you KISS. The point is: figure out how you KISS and start KISSing!

KISSing is crucial for leaving the rat race and enjoying life. To create excitement in your life, you need to liberate time and resources. Ditching your crap, and not buying new crap, is the express lane to living it up. Immerse yourself in pleasures, not payments!

But remember, we all have different perspectives. What may be meaningless to others may be meaningful to you. You decide what you keep and what you ditch. Don't let anyone else influence you.

Once you have finished purging, remember what my beloved Uncle Coco taught me: it is easy to buy but hard to sell. Once you have uncluttered your life, don't start buying more stuff. Be content with less. Ancient Roman Stoic philosopher and statesman Seneca said, "Until we have begun to go without them, we fail to realize how unnecessary many things are. We've been using them not because we needed them but because we had them."

The fewer things you have, the more you'll realize how unnecessary they were. For example, the best rule of thumb for discarding an item is: if you have not used it in six months, chuck it. I used 90 days, instead of six months, and got rid of a lot. I donated it all.

Learn to say good riddance. Don't fret about giving things up. Rejoice in liberation from ownership. And do not cheat. Organizing is not minimizing. Moving an item from your kitchen to the garage is not minimizing, it's passing the buck. Be honest, and don't kid yourself.

For example, I will share my rule for clothes with you. If they don't all fit in a steamer trunk, I have too much clothing. This strategy has simplified my wardrobe choices. I'm not at the Steve Jobs level yet. You know, jeans and black turtlenecks only. But I'm close and have saved a fortune in clothing costs. I've been buying from Ralph Lauren since I was a teenager, and now I do it online, so I don't even have to leave the house! Simplifying your attire is a great move for ejecting yourself from the rat race and thumbing your nose at the "required" uniform. But don't go haywire either.

I should add, the trunk trick may be easier for the guys than for the ladies. So, ladies can go for two trunks. That's fair. But no more. Again, no cheating.

Also remember that collections are for museums. Don't collect things, collect memories and experiences instead. Collect knowledge over knickknacks. Collect joy over junk. Get the drift?

"But, Art, I love my boat." My friend, keep it. Another idea—you can always rent one when the urge arises instead of buying one. Think about it. Let someone else worry about insurance, maintenance, and bank payments.

KISSing is not about depriving yourself of the things you enjoy, it's about simplifying the way you enjoy them. The easier things are, the more excitement they provide. And, I'd venture to say that renting that holy-cow, deluxe luxury item could provide a ton more pleasure than actually buying it.

An area that you'll definitely want to simplify is personal finance. Get rid of all those credit cards! Try to consolidate all your credit card debt into just one card. I highly recommend the Luxury Gold MasterCard from Barclays. I've had mine for years, and the advantages, incentives, and services are incredible. Truly exceptional. In the next book, we'll have a talk about saving and splurging, but for now, KISS those credit cards goodbye.

Another advantage of KISSing, of living with just enough, is that you free up time to look after yourself because you aren't dreaming or researching the next thing you "must have," "must buy." What happens, then, is that you have more time for walks, swims, making love, or whatever gets your blood pumping. You have more time for solitary reflection. You have more time to spend with your loved ones and to fortify your cherished relationships. Time is too precious to waste on trinkets.

Pastor and writer Rick Warren said, "The problem with stuff is, the more you have, the more it takes to take care of it all—the more you have to clean it, the more you have to protect it, the more you have to insure it, and the more you have to repair it." So, spend time on what matters. Enjoy the gifts God has sent your way, and send forth into the world those you no longer need.

The benefits of KISSing are amazing. You'll have more time, energy, and money, as you spend less on junk. You'll have more freedom and less stress. Your presence will have less environmental impact. You will be an excellent example of stewardship for your kids. Plus, the things you do buy can be of higher quality. You'll be able to afford more luxurious pleasures, such as exotic travel and decadent meals. Talk about an exceptional way to live.

Remember, less is more.

For me, the importance of KISSing is that I can be more charitable. Philanthropy is my life's cornerstone and mission. For example, through your RiosTalks.com membership, you're contributing to:

- The United Way
- The American Red Cross
- St. Jude's Children's Hospital
- Mercy Ships
- American Society for the Prevention of Cruelty to Animals (ASPCA)
- Doctors Without Borders

- Shriners Hospital
- SER de Puerto Rico
- Hindu Temple of Florida
- Project Smile
- St. Thomas' Church
- And more

I know they thank you for your support and generosity.

On that note, let me end by challenging you to simplify your life. Get rid of the clutter and enjoy life's pleasures. You'll have more to give to those with less, or as Gandhi said, "Live simply so others may simply live."

Until we talk again, stay happy and healthy, my friend.

**6**

## TAKEAWAYS

- KISSing is about keeping things simple. It's about decluttering, simplifying, and minimizing.

- Having less stuff is great. You will have fewer things to clean, maintain, fix, pay for, worry about, and obsess over.

- It's completely okay to want some things and to buy some of those things, just don't want and buy everything.

# Pandemics

*When written in Chinese, the word crisis*
*is composed of two characters.*
*One represents danger, and*
*the other represents opportunity.*
—JOHN F. KENNEDY

**Our planet is under attack.** Our enemy wants to kill every human on Earth. This villain has attacked over 17 million people and has killed over 667 thousand. And we cannot even see our enemy. It is invisible. The enemy is coronavirus, more specifically, COVID-19. As of this writing, we are in the throes of a worldwide pandemic. Let's talk.

While I hadn't considered writing about pandemics for this book, because this pandemic has so greatly affected everyone's lives, I started pondering how humans face adversity. And that is what this talk is about: conquering crises.

My entire family has stayed home together for more than four months now. For us, that's my two adult daughters, my wife, me, and our dogs, together in a modest-sized home. We have three bedrooms and a comfortable living space, but not a lot of extra breathing room. As you likely know all too well, it can be challenging to be forced to live in close quarters without the option to leave. And we'll stay together at home for at least several more weeks. My view—this is a positive thing, a significant opportunity.

Let me acknowledge that those who have lost loved ones to the virus will not see it this way. And that makes perfect sense. My heart goes out to everyone who has lost loved ones.

What I'm talking about here, though, is the opportunities a crisis, biological or not, can provide.

I am a firm believer in preordination—everything happens for a reason. Hence, the logic behind the Chinese symbol for crisis, danger and opportunity. Facing a crisis may present hazards of all kinds, but it also presents opportunities. During a crisis, you learn to survive outside the norm. When you face adversity, see it as an opportunity to learn novel ways to cope.

God never gives us more than we can handle. So, tackle each crisis as a blessing, as a challenge to your greatness. We're all great. Believe it, because time will judge your courage in the face of adversity.

After the crisis has passed, will you remember being brave or cowardly? I bet your memories will be of your bravery in tackling the challenge head-on. You'll thank God for giving you the opportunity although at first you thought it was a curse. You may cry now, but fight adversity with all your might because something good always comes out of something bad.

It's a matter of turning lemons into lemonade. I'll give you a marvelous example. If the virus had not hit, *Let's Talk* might have never come to pass. This project has been a dream of mine for years. But I would always find some lame excuse to put it off. Then the pandemic hit. I had some extra time, I had no excuses, and my passion for the project caught fire. God lit my fire.

Whether *Let's Talk* succeeds is in your hands. Without your support, it cannot flourish. But the talks wouldn't have a chance if I hadn't written this book. So, thank you for reading it and for helping *Let's Talk* flourish.

With that in mind, a crisis may be the push you need to tackle a project head-on or to overcome a barrier that is deterring your dreams. A crisis may present the opportunity for you to become truly exceptional. Something amazing came out of this crisis for me, and I'm praying the same will happen to you.

For example, a pandemic-like crisis is an excellent time for you to serve your neighbors, as prudently and safely as possible, because no matter how bad you may have it, someone else has it worse. Crises also allow us to reflect on what truly matters and to put aside the trivial. Leave behind grudges and reconcile. Forgive the relative who slighted you, be the bigger person and reach out to see if they need help. If your marriage has fizzled, spice it up. Relight the passion. This is the perfect time to take toll and fix things that may have needed fixing for a long time.

And remember, the only way to make lemonade is to cut lemons, squeeze them, add water and sugar, etc. In other words, you must have initiative and take action. You may think, "Sure, Art, but way easier said than done." My response—it's more fun to be a player than a spectator. And it's exceptional to be the light in the darkness.

As neuroscientist and author Abhijit Naskar said, "Be a live torch amidst the darkest night. If not you, who else will light up the society!" In a radical emergency, like a pandemic, you must be the light in the darkness for the people around you. A crisis is a perfect opportunity for parents to teach their children about adversity, to teach their kids to be the light in the darkness.

During this pandemic, our girls are home, as their universities went to distance learning. It has been amazing. We have loved every minute. Rather than get frustrated at the Wi-Fi crashing because we're all on it at once, or arguing over what to watch on TV, we have made lemonade out of the lemons the virus has been throwing at us. We've also used those lemons to make great rum and cokes!

But beyond the family time we've enjoyed, my girls haven't witnessed Sharon and me fall apart. They've seen us keep on trucking. Rather than freak out with anxiety and worry, stay in bed most of the day, all the while perusing the internet for any kind of information to feed fear and panic—and believe it or not, this bizarre coping strategy is one that people engage in—they've seen me make positive use of this time. They have seen me continue to work from home. They have seen me revamp the way the family law firm operates, so we don't skip a beat. And they've seen me finally make *Let's Talk* a reality.

My girls have also seen their mother maintain our household amid the mayhem. Provisions have been scarce, as grocery stores in our area haven't been well stocked and we haven't been allowed to go to them daily. As a result, my girls have seen Sharon use every single item in our pantry, from canned corned beef to cornstarch to popcorn.

Admittedly, there have been difficult days when everyone has preferred to do their own thing, fix their own meals, and eat by themselves. There have been days when family bonding has seemed like a drag. But there have been more days when Sharon made banquets for us, with a smile on her face and love in her heart—an incredible lasagna and an adobo chicken come to mind —and we gelled wonderfully when feasting together. In short, our daughters have learned to cope and persevere. When their time comes to face a crisis with their kids, they will have rugged memories to fall back on.

Shifting gears, a crisis is also a significant time to seek divine guidance. To ask for God's grace and intervention. It's the perfect time to strengthen your relationship with the Almighty. If your faith isn't strong, strengthen it. If it's already strong, it can only get stronger if you turn to God for nurturance.

In our talk on gratitude, we discussed thanking God when things are good, rather than consulting Him only when things are bad. But, you must turn to Him in adversity. Like any loving parent, He will be there for you. Knowing that God will get us through this pandemic has given me peace.

I also know that God helps those who help themselves. So you must be proactive and tackle problems head-on. A pandemic is nature's way of testing our mettle. And, my friend, the mere fact that you're reading this book tells me your mettle is fierce.

That's why a crisis is nothing more than the proverbial opportunity in disguise. It's a way for you to do things you have never done before. So dare to dream. Do things you have always wanted to do but were afraid to do.

We sometimes get into a rut and don't even know it. We let our dreams wither and our inner fire fizzle. We work, then go home, and are too tired to do anything else. We become zombies until the next morning, then do it all over again. The unexciting rat race. We don't push for more because we're lazy, because we're at a level of comfort that seems okay, or because we don't lack for anything material. This is not an easy way to live. There is no pleasure in living this way.

Then a crisis hits, you find yourself with extra time or even needing to revamp your income stream. At that moment, you must become fierce and relight your fire. Let your determination burn bright. Be the rock your family needs you to be. Inspire your community. Put on a cheery face and use every virtue you have to slay the enemy. And when you do, don't forget to congratulate yourself for your courage and to reward yourself with a few pleasures.

Also, remember that you don't have to face a crisis alone. You can rely on other people. Your spouse, kids, parents, siblings, and friends are sources of strength and support. There's strength in numbers. And there's strength in getting vulnerable and asking for help.

Crises are inevitable. They will come at you in many forms throughout your lifetime. When they do, you can be an ostrich and bury your head in the sand. Or you can be a lion and face the challenge head-on.

Learning to see crises as opportunities is a matter of perspective, and you are the sole master of your viewpoint. Choose greatness over mediocrity. Be a shepherd, not a sheep. Be exceptional.

You cannot allow a crisis, no matter what mask it wears, to curtail your happiness and enjoyment of life. Don't let a crisis stop you from enjoying your pleasures. Remember to welcome a crisis as an opportunity, not a calamity.

Crises are mere road bumps thrown in our paths to test our resolve. But they're just bumps, not mountains. You drive over them. Sure, you may need to slow down or take an alternate route, but you keep going until you make it around. A mere bump in the road doesn't stop your journey.

If you're reading this book, you're resilient. You are a fighter because this book is not for quitters. You have resolve and strength. Your desire to read this book means you want to expand your crisis fighting arsenal. And if you'd like to read more about things to do during a pandemic, visit www.RiosTalks.com and download a free copy of *Let's Talk: About 77 Exciting, Easy, and Inexpensive Things to Do During Trying Times*.

So, I pray that God will guide you through any crisis you may face. I pray that He will emblazon you with the courage and strength you'll need for victory. But promise me, and yourself, that you will never give up.

As always, I leave you with a great quote, this one from golfing legend Jack Nicklaus, who said, "Crises are part of life. Everybody has to face them, and it doesn't make any difference what the crisis is."

Until we talk again, stay happy and healthy, my friend.

**7** **TAKEAWAYS**

- God never gives us more than we can handle.

- Don't allow a crisis to curtail your happiness and enjoyment of life.

- Welcome a crisis as an opportunity, not a calamity.

# The One Wine Lunch

*Ask not what you can do for your country.*
*Ask what's for lunch.*
—ORSON WELLES

**Who the hell drinks** three martinis at lunch? Well, Orson Welles did! He was a genius and world-class bon vivant. To Mr. Welles, lunch was just as important as serving your country. Okay, that may be a tad much, but you get the gist. Let's talk.

I'm a lunch lover. It is the highlight of my day, and I'm fanatic about it. Lunch is generally my biggest meal, my daily banquet. And one wine lunches are sublime.

Apologies, Mr. Welles, but the three-martini lunch is insane. Who can drink them and go back to work? I can't. President Ford was a big proponent of the three-martini lunch. That's scary.

I don't know about three martinis, but a glass of wine before lunch sure seems civilized. Hemingway said that wine is one of the most civilized things in the world. Who'll argue with Papa? Wine is refined, and what better time to enjoy a glass—yes, one single glass—than at lunch? Hence, the one wine lunch.

It's a great stress-releaser and will increase your productivity and creativity. Taking a break for lunch, away from work, makes all the sense in the world. You literally leave the rat race, for at least an hour. It makes your life easier. So go have a pleasant lunch. I am not talking about going to a Michelin star restaurant. You can go to a great food truck, as long as it sells wine or beer!

Have a nice glass of wine before you eat lunch. It will bolster your inventiveness, as wine tends to do. But more than anything, it relaxes your mind. Give yourself that midday pause. A pleasure indeed.

In Europe, it is reasonable to have a glass of wine before lunch. In the States, it once was considered sensible to have a drink over lunch. Today, if anybody sees you having a drink during lunch, they'll think you have a drinking problem. That has nothing to do with it. Totally off the mark. Having a glass of wine at lunch is not irresponsible at all. It calms you.

The best "stratagem" is to go out for lunch. If you can't afford to go to a restaurant every day, it's okay. But do leave your workplace during lunch. Make your day easier for a bit and take that break. Pack a lunch and a single-serving wine bottle. If you can, go to a restaurant. Sit back and relax while you wait for your food. That's the time to enjoy a glass of wine.

As far as company during lunchtime goes, that may vary. I like to have lunch by myself sometimes. I need solitude now and then. On other occasions, I'll call my wife, Sharon, to see if she'll join me. If she does, we enjoy a glass of wine before lunch.

I also love having lunch with my parents. We work together, so we have lunch together often. Being able to see my parents almost daily is a blessing I cherish.

After lunch, if you still have a little time, sit in a park or go for a brief walk. Get some fresh air. Being outside provides perspective about the world around you. You'll notice other people going about their lives, which reminds you that we all have a purpose.

I hope you don't think the one wine lunch idea is insane. How about this? Pause for a sec and do a quick little internet search. Type "one wine lunch" and check out what pops up. What you'll find—there are many people, much smarter than me, that say this is a superb idea. It's a simple way to make your life easier every day at noon.

People who say that they're too busy to have lunch have a misguided sense of their importance. Anyone can take a lunch break. Even if it's a half-hour. Step away, have a meal, and relax. First, not doing it is counter-productive. To have your mind working nonstop for eight hours is not healthy. Even race cars take breaks. They can't go full rev for eight hours, they need pit stops. Your mind and body are more complex than a race car, so you need pit stops also.

Looking at it health-wise, having something to eat at lunch gives you energy. It keeps your blood sugar levels where they should be. I am not a doctor or health expert. That's the last thing I am! But this makes sense. There's proof that people who don't eat lunch gain weight because they overeat at dinner. Plus, it messes up the metabolism, really slowing it down. Not only that, but your energy will wane if you don't have lunch. Back to the race car, if you don't gas it up, it stalls. We need gas also. I like to gas up with food and wine—just one glass—at lunch.

I am sure that somebody out there is wondering, "If one glass of wine at lunch is good, aren't two better?" How is this for a lawyerly answer: it depends. If you're on vacation, or you don't have to go back to work, or if it's the weekend, sure, have two glasses. Three, as long as you're not driving. Having one glass of wine before you eat your lunch shouldn't impair anyone to the point they can't drive. But, if one glass impairs you, do not drive! Uber.

I have my glass of wine before I eat lunch. I don't drink anything while I eat, not even water. So by the time I finish lunch, I'm fine and dandy. By the way, that's not science. It's my logic, so don't take my word for it. Again, if you have a glass of wine and cannot drive afterward, do not drive. Walk to the restaurant, kill two birds with one stone.

If you have to go back to work, then what about that second glass? Be honest and responsible. You're not going to be as sharp. But if you're having a lazy afternoon, there's nothing wrong with having the second glass. Or if it's a social lunch with a friend, or you're celebrating something special, live it up. Yet again, use your common sense. Be responsible and moderate. Trust your instinct and do the right thing.

As we were talking about happy hour in a previous talk, the one wine lunch is a teaser for happy hour. They go together. You know, like mac and cheese, Batman and Robin, rum and coke, chips and salsa, Scooby and Shaggy, one wine lunch and happy hour.

The one wine lunch—I hope you'll see the merit in it and allow yourself this pleasure. A little excitement and self-indulgence at lunch is wonderful. So, take your lunch break. Do it consistently, responsibly, and methodically. Make it a consistent ritual. You don't necessarily have to do it every day, like happy hour. It's just better more often than not. Go out for lunch, have a glass of wine, relax a bit, and get away from the daily grind. It'll be miraculous for your mind, body, and soul.

As always, I'll leave you with a great quote: as journalist and writer Waverley Root said, "Drink wine every day, at lunch and dinner, and the rest will take care of itself."

Until we talk again, stay happy and healthy, my friend.

## 8   TAKEAWAYS

- Wine is refined, and what better time to enjoy a glass—yes, one single glass—than at lunch?

- Anyone can take a lunch break. Step away, have a glass of wine, eat a nice meal, and relax. Even race cars take breaks.

- A little excitement and self-indulgence at lunch is wonderful.

# Be Extra, But Not Extravagant

*My dad's greatest strength is being extra,*
*and his greatest weakness is being extra!*
—MARIA F. RIOS

**You should maximize life's experiences,** but not overpay for them. It's okay to be extra, but not extravagant. Confused? Let's talk.

I recently overheard my daughters talking about me. Maria told Alondra that my biggest strength was "being extra," but that it was also my biggest weakness. Hmm. What does that mean, "being extra"? And how could it be a strength and a weakness?

To my daughters' generation, millennials, "being extra" means "a bit too much" or "a little over the top." But it does not mean extravagant. Extravagant means "without restraint in spending money or using resources."

So, extra means buying a $100,000 car while extravagant means buying a $500,000 car. Everything is relative, but you get the point. What I'm proposing is that—metaphorically (or literally, depending on your income or debt level!)—you buy the $100,000 car even though you could buy the $500,000 car. Be extra, but not extravagant.

Just to be clear—I'm not contradicting Talk #6 about keeping things simple. Remember that KISSing is not about depriving yourself. KISSing is about decluttering, simplifying, and avoiding excess.

Being extra means you allow yourself pleasures— quality pleasures. And if other people don't approve, who cares? Screw 'em! They need to mind their own beeswax anyway. Even better, they need to dig deeper and get some Zen in their life, so they can learn not to give a crap about other people's business.

What I'm saying is that you should add a little extra "oomph" to your life. Add extra spice to your pleasure, but don't break the bank.

I have seen both sides of this plot. Some misers never spend, saving everything because they think they'll live forever. On the other end are the wasters, who believe they'll die tomorrow, so they might as well spend it all today. They're both wrong. Many people have become rich by living poorly while others have become poor by living richly. But there is no need to go to extremes. You can be extra without breaking the bank, and you can preserve the bank by not being extravagant. I learned the dangers of these two extremes from my grandfathers.

On the one hand, was my maternal grandfather, Papote. He was the grandest bon vivant who ever lived. At his funeral, I heard two of his closest friends talking. One told the other, "He went on to a better life," and the other replied, "Impossible! It can't get better than the one he lived!" Although Papote left his family well-off, he went through at least four fortunes in his lifetime. Ah, but he enjoyed every second to the fullest. And I mean, big time!

Then there was my paternal grandfather, Abuelito. He was the most honorable and righteous man I ever met. But he was tight with the dollar, if you get my drift. He had a sign by the phone that read, "Telephones are for shortening distances, not for prolonging conversations." Abuelito watched the pennies. That's why he left so many dollars when he passed.

But who lived a fuller life? Again, everything is relative. Abuelito's pleasure was in living a prudent life. And yet, I'm sure he wouldn't have minded going on a few Papote-style romps.

I don't think you need to pick a camp here. There is a middle ground—and it's a glorious location—but my grandfathers never learned this lesson.

Please take note: again, I'm not suggesting being irresponsible. You must save before you splurge. You never want to get into impossible, ridiculous, or even dangerous debt. You can't blow it all on today's party because there'll be another one tomorrow.

That brings me to the importance of being extra, of living a little over the top. At times and in select ways. I know that when I near my end, I will not reminisce about my dull days. Instead, I'll relive my days of debauchery, my "moveable feasts," to coin Hemingway. But it's not over yet. I'll be making memories until I die.

And that is my advice to you. Make extraordinary memories. Be extra, my friend. Splurge on extra nice things. Imelda Marcos said, "People say I'm extravagant because I want to be surrounded by beauty. But tell me, who wants to be surrounded by garbage?" Granted, Mrs. Marcos was known to go on $7 million shopping sprees and she had around 3 thousand pairs of shoes, but still, the lady had a point.

Why live a wasted life? Why surround yourself with garbage instead of beauty? I am not suggesting you become a dictator and pilfer your country's wealth. But it's okay to indulge, to be extra.

Remember, misers are never happy, but I've never seen a depressed bon vivant. Keep it in moderation. Allow yourself luxuries, without going overboard.

For example, you don't have to eat the $20 steak if you can afford the $50 steak. But, even if you can afford it, there's no reason to eat the $100 steak.

You don't have to force down the $10 bottle of wine when you can get the $30 bottle. But still, don't even look at the $90 bottle. We all know where the wine is going to wind up anyway! I actually solve this problem by buying all my wine through Wine.com, where I get incredible deals on very nice bottles.

You don't have to travel coach if you can go first class. But you don't have to charter a private jet either. You get the gist here. Don't blow your paycheck on any one thing. But, don't put everything in the bank either. Investing in your experiences is investing in your memories.

There is a caveat to this: you need to allow yourself at least one or two grand extravagances in your life. Not extras, I'm talking big enchilada extravagances. If you have a dream item, one you've always wanted—a fancy car, a vacation home, a luxurious trip—if you can afford it, go for it. You need to get it out of your system, love it, and then move on with life.

Here is an alternative. Don't buy the toys; rent them! Want an exotic car? Rent one for a week. You'll be over it by then. Want a yacht? Charter one in the Caribbean. After a week, you'll be tired of lobster. A villa in Tuscany? Lease one for two weeks. You may be homesick by then. But, if you must, buy your one or two extravagant blow-out toys.

So, what is your dream toy? What is your big dog, top banana bucket list item? Whatever it is, I'll say a prayer on your behalf tonight. It's okay to pray for what we want, as long as we give thanks and pray for others first. After all, dreams are the seeds of the flowers of reality. So dream and plant that seed. Your hard work, success, and determination will make it come true.

But, there is a caveat to allowing yourself a big-and-bad extravagance: something must give. If you buy your dream boat, forego the dream car, drive a Ford instead of a Ferrari. If you're buying your dream house, you can do without the vacation home. I don't believe in vacation homes anyway; they limit your choice of places to travel. The bottom line—get your one or two extravagant toys, but be moderate in other areas. Remember, you can always rent the toys!

And this brings us to the pinnacle of this talk: giving. If God's blessings allow you to be extra, be extra. But give extravagantly. Remember to give before you get. Of course, crazy give to your family, friends, favorite charities, and colleagues. But there's so many people to give extravagantly to—the barista, the mailman, the waiter, the cashier, the garbage collector, the person standing behind you in line, the street musician, the person twirling the sign on the corner in the summer sun. And yes, every single beggar you come across. Give them a coffee, a doughnut, a ten-dollar bill, a cold drink, a big smile, a high five. Give and spread the joy of life. Giving is one of life's exceptional pleasures.

Not that it matters, but to remind you—everything you give comes back to you tenfold. That's not why you should give, but it can be a motivator. A little icing on the giving cake.

I will let you go now, to be extra, but not extravagant. Live the days of wine and roses, just don't buy the most expensive ones every time. But do buy the nicer ones!

Oh—and one more thing: I think my daughter Maria said that being extra was both my greatest strength and weakness because I give to a fault, but I also spend to a fault. Don't worry, Maria, I'm working on it!

As always, I leave you with a quote from one wiser than me. As moral philosopher Bernard Williams said, "An extravagance is something that your spirit thinks is a necessity," and for the sake of this chapter, substitute in the word "extra" for Mr. Williams' "extravagance."

Until we talk again, stay happy and healthy, my friend.

## 9 TAKEAWAYS

- Being extra means you allow yourself quality pleasures. Add a little extra "oomph" to your life, just don't break the bank.

- Misers are never happy, but I've never seen a depressed bon vivant. Allow yourself luxuries, without going overboard.

- You need to allow yourself at least one or two grand extravagances in your life. Not extras, but big enchilada extravagances.

# Logging Off

*I think people spend too much time staring into screens, and not enough time drinking wine, tongue kissing, and dancing under the moon.*

—RACHEL WOLCHIN

**Pause for a moment** to imagine somebody and their drone—the drone is out there flying around and having a great time in the sunshine while its person stands immobile, staring at a screen, as if in some kind of trance. It's like the person is the machine while the drone is out there hootin' and hollerin' and living it up. I love technology, but it seems like instead of us working it, it's working us. My argument—we have to go off the grid every now and then. We can't let the drones enjoy our lives for us. We need to log off. Let's talk.

Why should we regularly set our technology aside? Because, like Rachel Wolchin said, when we're constantly stuck in our screens, we're missing out on the magical stuff that's happening around us. The real world, the trees, the clouds, the people around us. Forget virtual reality—what's happening around us, and within us, that's actual reality, and we're missing it. We're missing it simply because we're crouched over staring at our screens. We forget to put down our devices and look around to experience real life.

Sure, you might be thinking, "Going offline is fine. It's okay to do that." My response—it's more than fine, going offline is divine. Walking away from your smartphone, choosing not to check emails, turning off notifications, and simply being where you're at—now that's divine. Whether you're alone or with loved ones, your dog, your parakeet, or flowers and trees, it is divine to log off and experience those around you and your environment. It is luxurious to our senses and to our very soul.

By disconnecting from the ever-whirling devices, we reconnect with ourselves. I don't mean in some heavy, existential, angsty kind of way. I mean reconnecting with ourselves to reconnect with our delights, our memories, our dreams and plans, and our very experience of the present moment in a natural and satisfying way. It provides a refreshing and de-stressing dip into the fresh lake of life. It also means reconnecting with the people around us, our loved ones, family, and friends.

It's a massive irony that as we've become obsessed with being constantly accessible and available to everyone—colleagues, extended family, friends from college, high school, and even grade school—we've become inaccessible to ourselves and even to the ones we love the most.

In our desperation to read and respond to the never-ending electronic beeps, we've become less known, even unknown and inaccessible to the very loved ones that we share our homes with. And them to us. It's a sad two-way street of inaccessibility. Something got lost. But it's something we can all find again by making some strategic decisions around logging off.

The first step in retaking yourself, your life, and your loved ones, is to realize the truth. To realize that it's perfectly fine and divine to go offline. The world's not going to end if you go off-grid for a bit. The world isn't going to explode because you turned off your phone or laptop. The sun will rise again. When you log back on, the world will still be there. Writer Anne Lamott said, "Almost everything will work again if you unplug it for a few minutes, including you." That is so important. I read somewhere that when you put down your phone, you pick up your life. Isn't it about time you pick up your life?

The first step is to internalize that it's fine to go offline. You won't lose your place in the world. And once you practice it and get good at it, I predict you'll move a step farther from thinking, "It's fine," to realizing, "It's divine!" The more you log off, the more you'll realize how fabulously freeing it truly is.

So how do you do it? I don't recommend being random about it. Be strategic in logging off. I have set times of the day, times of the week, and even physical spaces as tech-free. But before we go into the strategy, I can already predict a sticking point that we need to address ASAP.

The big sticking point: emergencies. The biggest reason most people are afraid to unplug is that there could be an emergency. It's impossible to find the joy and freedom that can come from unplugging, if all the while, you're afraid that someone important in your life, like your spouse or child, has an emergency and can't reach you. And the reality is that emergencies happen. Especially if you have children, no matter how old they are, you want to be available in case they call with an emergency.

To account for the reality of emergencies, I've got a contingency plan. It's called the second phone. The second phone is a very simple, old-school, low-tech cell

phone whose only feature is the phone itself. No internet. No texting. Just calls. And you give out that phone
number only to the few people who are most important
in your life—like your spouse, children, parents, and
siblings—those who if they have an emergency, you
want to know about it immediately. In my case, it's only
my wife, my parents, my sister, and my two daughters
that have the second phone number. No one else.

What's the point of the second phone? When you're
armed with that second phone, you can go off the grid,
but technically you're still on it. You're ninety-nine percent
off the grid. That one percent is your second phone that
is always on and with you, so you're accessible to your
select loved ones in case of an emergency.

Yeah, sure, it's cheating. You aren't off the grid. But,
it gives you the needed peace of mind in case there's an
emergency. It's cheating for a good cause! And take note
that for all the following tips I'm giving you on how to
log off and enjoy tech-free spaces and times of day, you
should still have your second phone on and with you.
It is cheating, but it also allows you to let go and fully
embrace your (practically) tech-free time!

With that said, let's talk about how to go tech-free.
Equipped with that private line, that second phone, one
of the things that I love to do is leave my (main) cell

phone in the car when I get home from work. That would be the cell where I get texts, emails, voicemails, all that good stuff. I don't bring it into the house. If I'm working from home, at five o'clock, I turn off that cell, and—catch this—I won't turn it on until nine o'clock the next morning.

Oh my gosh, I cannot tell you how freeing that is. It's just such a relief. It's like the bell going off at the factory when it's quitting time. I always think of the *Flintstones*, when the bell goes off and Fred goes flying home.

For you—leave your main phone in the car. Or if you work from home, turn it off. And remember, because you have that second low-tech phone, you have peace of mind.

When else should you turn off your phone, leave it in the car, or leave it at home? When you go out on a date, whether with your longtime spouse or on a first-time date or even on a family outing—don't bring it. Give your undivided attention to the person you're with. Stare into their twinkling eyes. Take in the sights, sounds, and smells of the venue. Dwell on the taste and texture of your food and drink. Get tactile and sensual with the experience. I love to go on no-phone dates with Sharon.

When you go to a movie, the theater, a musical, a show, a play—don't bring your main phone with you.

Checking a phone is rude to the people around you, but it's also distracting to you. It keeps you chained to the office, to your so-called buddies, and to the device itself, so that you're not present with yourself and your surroundings. You're not relaxed and immersed. If you're in the theater, relax and enjoy the movie. When you walk the dog, leave the phone at home. On lazy Sundays, why in the world would you have your phone on? You don't want to be looking at emails. You don't want to be looking at texts, nothing. Certainly if you want to make a few real calls to friends and family to catch up and connect, that's wonderful. But that's not the same as getting into a screen trance.

Remember when we talked about happy hour? Happy hours, as I mentioned, are tech-free. You don't want any interruptions in your happy hour. That's a no-brainer. My favorite way to exercise is swimming. Obviously you're not going to swim with your cell phone. But I notice a lot of swimmers at the pool have their phones close by. Nope, not in my case. Again, my main cell phone is in my car. Not poolside. When you work out, whether you go to a gym, go for a walk, or you're doing some Tai Chi in the backyard, have your emergency second phone nearby. Of course, some people like to jog with music, that's fine. But put it in airplane mode, so you only hear music and don't get calls or texts that could disturb your mind space while exercising.

This may sound extremely old-fashioned, but when I'm driving, I don't even like to have the radio on. I love tech-free car rides. If I'm driving to the office, my radio is off. And I'm just thinking about what's going to be happening that day. In a very broad sense. Just kind of visualizing what I want to happen (something we'll explore in the next talk on power vision). A tech-free commute is incredibly relaxing. I love to roll the windows down, have the radio off, and get some fresh air. For a longer drive, maybe I'll put on an audiobook or satellite radio, and listen to some very chill music. No words. Instrumental. In the car I'm going either no-tech or very low-tech. Texts, emails, anything like that is not for the car. Not only does it keep you chained to the office and to the apparatus itself, it's simply dangerous. It can wait.

What about lunchtime? We've already discussed the energy-boosting and utterly sensual getaway that the one wine lunch provides during the workday. To make it as glorious as it should be, remember this: absolutely no technology during lunch. For the love of God. By lunchtime, we've been hustling and up to our ears in all things screen and tech—and soon enough we'll be back on the hamster wheel, sweating away in front of our screens, so let's allow ourselves that tiny power break away from it all. We've got our second phone for emergencies, so no worries there. Anything work-related can wait for our return to work. Relish in it. Live it up by logging off.

Another staggering strategy is the no-tech bedroom. In your bedroom, you shouldn't have technology at all. Sure, you can have your second phone for emergencies, but other than that, nothing at all. No computer or TV for shows or movies. No smart tablets or phones. Nothing. Indeed, the no-tech bedroom negates the potential issue around devices emitting unsafe electromagnetic radiation and blue light that could interfere with the body's circadian rhythms. Reality is, the tech-free bedroom is more than that. It's about creating a special, maybe even sacred, space for you to wind down. To totally relax. To be away and uplifted.

Sharon and I have a no-tech bedroom (of course, the second phone is there, but in a drawer). The only thing that's going to happen in that bedroom is going to be sleep, the hanky-panky, and reading books. By reading books, I mean actual paper books. I don't read ebooks in my bedroom. I love to read traditional paperback and hard-back books. I love ebooks though, don't get me wrong. But I do ebooks for vacations, for plane rides, where I don't want to be lugging a bunch of books around because I'm usually reading about three or four books at a time. At home in the bedroom, it's real books.

The no-tech bedroom is a wonderful thing. Once you are there, you have a sacred getaway space. Sleeping, lovemaking, reading—grand and luxurious things.

Let's end this talk with a challenge. A huge challenge. My friend, I challenge you to take a digital-free vacation. Can you go on vacation and go completely tech-free? Can you log off? Again, remember that you can have that second phone, that emergency private line. You can have it with you 24/7. That's fine. In case of an emergency only. But beyond that, dare to go on vacation without looking at emails, texts, or anything like that. Dare to immerse yourself in the lush, ambrosial experiences of a vacation without the digital leash. I predict you'll find that it is utterly divine. I challenge you to do this.

While it might seem foreign or scary at first, choosing to go offline for a lunch, a happy hour, a night, a lazy Sunday, or even a vacation, after you've dipped your toe in, you'll discover that it is pure pleasure letting go of all that techno chatter. Remove the shackles of constantly being on call. Allow yourself to be present to the people around you, to the grass between your toes, to the rain on your upturned collar, or to the dog tugging at the leash. It's powerful to choose yourself, your life, and your loved ones over the beeping and flashing apparatus. Yes, it's definitely a choice that makes your life exciting, easier, and exceptional.

I'll wind down as I usually do with a quote on our topic. Musician, singer, and songwriter Jonathan Cain said, "We get sucked into the internet and streaming information, and it's time to just unplug and look within."

Until we talk again, stay happy and healthy, my friend.

## 10  TAKEAWAYS

- When we're constantly stuck in our screens, we're missing out on what's happening around us and within us.

- Establish regular time windows or places when you'll be logged off. I turn my main cell off from 5 pm to 9 am, and my bedroom is tech-free.

- Embrace logging off as a luxurious and invigorating expression of freedom and power. Because it is.

# Power Vision

*Everything you want is out there*
*waiting for you to ask. Everything you want*
*also wants you. But you have to take action*
*to get it.*
—JACK CANFIELD

**"Power vision."** If this phrase conjures up images of a superhero using superpowers, well, you may not be too far from the truth. Let's talk.

What I call "power vision" is the powerful effect that comes from visualizing something that you want to happen, believing in it, practicing that visualization, and then—*shazam!*—like a superpower, it becomes true. All you have to do is imagine what you want, envision it, and believe. Sure, this might sound a little hippy dippy, but you should know by now that I'm a pragmatic person. Please, hear me out.

I call it "power vision" because I find it a fun, engaging phrase. Others call it the Law of Attraction. In her book *The Secret*, Rhonda Byrne names this same envisioning phenomenon "the secret." Esther and Jerry Hicks have written quite a bit about it. They're probably at the forefront of the whole movement.

At the end of the day, power vision—or whatever name you prefer to call it—comes down to believing in your vision, and if you think it, believe it, and say it enough, it'll come true.

In essence, power vision is about imagining what you want, repeating it to yourself with words, and regularly visualizing it with mental imagery. By doing this recurrently and truly believing in it and your ability to have and achieve it, eventually the universe will make it happen.

If this seems whacky or hokey, think of this—we already spend a ton of time getting lost in our thinking. It's called daydreaming. Since we're already spending a lot of time daydreaming, there's nothing to lose by being more purposeful in it and actively envisioning the exceptional things we want for ourselves, our loved ones, and our world. You really have nothing to lose by trying this. So let's talk about how it works.

Power Vision 101: think about what it is that you want to happen. Let's say, for example, that I really want this book to get out there. I want *Let's Talk* to be successful because I want you, your friends, and everybody out there to become my friends through the book and to share in our conversation. So, let's say that for my power vision I want *Let's Talk* to reach X number of people, one way or another, be it through the book, the website club, *Let's Talk* live events and webinars, or the courses.

So, once you decide your what, like I did in the example, the next step is to do the envisioning. For me, I find a nice place—lying in bed in the morning, driving in the car, something like that—and I take whatever it is I've identified as my power vision and imagine it as if it's already happened.

For the *Let's Talk*-becoming-a-hit example, I'd come up with my affirmation statement—"*Let's Talk, Book 1* has reached X number of people"—and I'd repeat that to myself several times and then visualize how my life would look and feel as if it's already happened. I'd envision sharing emails with you and many others, talking with you on the phone, webinars, or at live events, and discussing how to make life exciting, easier, and exceptional. I'd envision loads of people contacting me with stories of how their lives have expanded and gotten even more grand as a result of our talks.

Side note: most proponents of the Law of Attraction recommend that you see what you want as if it's already happened, that what you're visualizing is already done. However, Michael J. Losier, bestselling author, NLP practitioner, and Law of Attraction coach, has a slightly different take on this. He believes that if you make your affirmation as if it's already happened, when in reality it hasn't happened yet, it makes you a little incredulous, so it doesn't work as well. What he recommends is saying, "I'm in the process of … [whatever it is you're trying to manifest]." So, that's another option, using Mr. Losier's way of framing your power vision, if that's more appealing to you. But again, the majority of experts believe that it's better if you envision your desire as if it's already happened.

Let's take another example. Say your goal is to become healthier, to both feel and look healthier. To practice this power vision, when you open your eyes in the morning, while still lying in bed, you could go into your mind's eye and see yourself living out your coming day in your healthier mind and body. You could see yourself and imagine the feeling of what it's like to zip up the stairs, to carry several bags of groceries in both your hands at once, and to stop eating when you're almost full, even if your plate isn't empty. You could envision the thirty minutes of swimming you'd be doing several times a week. You could envision your fridge and pantry filled with health-promoting, yet scrumptious, foods.

Maybe some of you want to manifest meeting the love of your life. You can use your power vision for that. Then visualize living a joyful, satisfying life with that person that you love. See yourself with your soulmate sitting next to you.

As Rhonda Byrne wrote in *The Secret*, "See the things that you want as already yours." That is the perfect summary of how power vision works.

But remember, for power vision to work, you have to have a very defined goal, a specified wish that you want to happen. To ensure this, there's two things that you can do. One: you can make a list. Make a list of things that you would like to have happen in your life, and then start making affirmations and power visions based on that list. Two: make a vision board. A vision board is nothing more than preparing a little poster and arranging pictures and/or written phrases on it that depict what you want to happen in your life. You arrange those on the poster in a visually appealing way. At first, a vision board might seem over the top, but I put in the effort to make one, and I found it fun. So whether you make a list or a vision board, the point is to identify in a specific way your power visions.

Something else to keep in mind is that when you do the visualizing, you should only work on one, maybe two, power visions at a time. If you try to envision, say, all 27 things you want for yourself in a single visualizing session, it won't work. It's like you're watering it all down, so nothing ends up happening.

Remember, you must really want what you're putting on that list or vision board. You must believe that it can happen because doubt kills your power vision. Doubting is like putting a lid on the power vision, so it won't happen. Because the way this works is simple—you ask, you believe, and you receive. It's that simple. Ask + Believe = Receive. As Esther and Jerry Hicks said, "There is nothing you cannot be, do, or have."

Now obviously, be realistic. You can't manifest that you want to fly like Superman because that's not going to happen. You can't ask the Law of Attraction to supersede the laws of physics. Don't limit your aspirations, but make them realistic, things that can physically happen. If you ask for what you want, and you really, really work on your affirmations and genuinely believe in them, they will happen.

BIG WARNING—*caution!*—the Law of Attraction and your power vision will not distinguish between good and bad thoughts, in other words, good and bad affirmations. You need to be extremely careful with your thoughts because if you're thinking that something negative will happen, it will happen. If you expect bad things to happen, they're going to happen because you're envisioning them. You're engaging in mental effort to see and expect them. Your power vision is seeing the bad thing and it thinks that's what you want, so that's what's going to happen.

I'm going to share something that now, years later, I actually attribute to me thinking negative thoughts. When I was younger, before I went to law school, I had a business that failed. Actually, that's why I went to law school, because this business failed. I started a business, and it was very innovative. I started the first mail-order pharmacy in Puerto Rico. I figured it would be grand because what could be more convenient than that? However, I did not expect that the local pharmacy owners would put up such a stink. I mean, of course, competition is competition, but I never thought it would get as nasty as it did.

In the end, the other pharmacy owners outfought me. Admittedly, they were sneaky, and I wasn't willing to compromise my ethics. I wasn't going to play dirty. So, unfortunately, the business failed and I had to declare bankruptcy, which to this day hurts. (I'm going to talk about this again in Talk #14.) But the point here is that while all this was happening, while I was embroiled in this fight against all these pharmacy owners, I kept thinking of the worst outcome. "If my business fails, what's going to happen?" I kept visualizing failure. Many different scenarios of failure.

I believe, to this day, that the power vision worked, but, in this case, it worked in the negative aspect. Why? Because the Law of Attraction doesn't differentiate between good and bad. It works based on what you're thinking. I now believe that if I had thought in a more positive sense, the outcome would have been different. Then again, I also believe that everything happens for a reason and that my failure had to happen so that my life would take a different path and bring me to where you and I are right now at this very moment.

Anyway, the point here is to be careful what you think about. Think positive things. Think about the good things you want to happen in your life, and they'll happen. Control your negative thoughts. And never wish ill on anybody else either, but that goes without saying!

Now, as far as the Law of Attraction and your power vision go, once you've come up with what you want to manifest, don't worry too much about how it's going to happen. Instead, put in regular effort doing your envisioning. In *Key to Living the Law of Attraction*, Jack Canfield wrote, "Our job is not to figure out the how. The how will show up out of the commitment and belief in the what." Simply believe in what you want to happen, and the universe will take care of the how.

If your power vision is mighty enough, it's going to happen. God will take care of the how. And when your power vision does come to fruition, acknowledge the miracle. Give credit where credit is due, and acknowledge the strength of your power vision practice. This is important.

Another important aspect of power vision is that you want to be surrounded by positivity, positive thoughts, positive people, positive places. If the people around you are negative, that's going to really put a damper on your power vision. Yes, it can be hard if it's a family member who is negative because you can't just ditch them. I recommend having a chat, saying to them, "Listen, let's be positive. We can't stay on this negative track. It's bringing me down, and it's bringing you down. It's no way to live. We can do and be better." Keep positivity and positive vibes around you all the time.

When I've talked to others about power vision, some have told me, "That's kind of greedy and selfish." My response—no, not true. There's nothing greedy about power vision. I promote looking at life from an abundance, not a scarcity, perspective. As I see it, there's an overabundance of everything in the universe. There's infinite love to go around. Believe me, there's also more than enough money and prosperity to go around. There's plenty of everything to go around. God is always going to create more of whatever we may need. So don't worry about thinking that power vision is about selfishness or greed.

One of my go-to power visions is visualizing the world being a better place, a more peaceful place, with people getting along, and our divisions just disappearing. I visualize people who look different from one another, who practice different religions and speak with differing accents, coming together and hanging out, helping each other, dancing, laughing, and telling stories. The point is that we can use power vision not just to manifest greater health, wealth, and happiness in our own lives, but in the world as a whole. Remember to use your power vision for others. After all, as discussed in our talk on gratitude, we've got to give to receive.

Before closing, let's spend a moment talking about ideal times to practice your power vision. I've already mentioned taking a moment first thing in the morning—right after you wake up and after you say words of gratitude for the blessings in your life, you can lie in bed an extra minute or two and take one of your power visions and do a full-on mental exploration of it. Another great time is during your morning commute, but keep your eye on the road! See it, hear it, feel it, taste that power vision. Any time you're alone, seize it as an opportunity to do some power visioning. Remember: Ask + Believe = Receive.

As always, I'd like to leave you with a really good quote. It's from Buddha who said, "All that we are is the result of what we have thought."

Until we talk again, stay happy and healthy, my friend.

**11**

# TAKEAWAYS:

- If your power vision is mighty enough and you sincerely believe in it, it's going to happen. Remember: Ask + Believe = Receive.

- Because the Law of Attraction doesn't differentiate between good and bad, be careful what you think about. Think positive things.

- If you want your power vision to manifest, remember, you have to give to receive.

# 100 Hours of Solitude

*The more powerful and original a mind,*
*the more it will incline towards the*
*religion of solitude.*
—ALDOUS HUXLEY

**You may have read** Gabriel García Márquez's book *One Hundred Years of Solitude*. Well—hold your horses! I'm not proposing you spend a hundred years alone, but I do see spending a hundred hours alone, every now and then, as a great thing. I bet you're thinking, "Art, that sounds a little (or a lot) antisocial," but actually, it's not. Let's talk.

To clarify, I'm not promoting a hundred hours alone on a mountaintop. Or in a cave. Or walking on your knees across a briar patch. Nothing insane like that. I'm not even recommending one of those Vipassana silent retreats, though they sound interesting. What I am recommending is setting aside a hundred hours, which is about four days, by yourself, two or three times a year. You take some time off, a four-day weekend, away from work, away from the family, away from everybody. During the four days, you go off on your own to a nice, quiet place and spend some time pretty much in seclusion. Why? To catch up with yourself, with your plans, goals, and dreams. To think, be, read, envision. To check in with yourself and chill out. After all, as French existentialist Albert Camus put it, "In order to understand the world, one has to turn away from it on occasion."

The first key for your four-day "solitude sojourn," as I like to call it, is to find an ideal tranquil spot away from home. For me, it's about getting away from the big city and going to a rural and remote place. A natural setting. I'm really into it, so I rent a small, one-room, open-plan log cabin on a farm about a 12-hour drive from home. It's right outside of a quaint little town. I go into town and have a nice lunch—you know I like my lunches—and grab dinner for the night. Other than that, I spend time in the cabin.

It's quite a long drive for me to get up to the farm. But for me, the drive is part of the hundred-hours-of-solitude experience. I split up the drive, spending a night in a hotel on the way and then continuing the next day. I think a long drive is great during your solitude sojourn because it allows you time alone with your thoughts. If I have music playing when I drive, it's going to be soothing and calm, maybe some smooth jazz. I'm not listening to the news or even to songs that bring back memories because that's a distraction. That takes me out of myself and the present moment.

You already know I'm going to say this, but don't think that'll stop me. Seeing as the whole point of the solitude sojourn is to reacquaint yourself with yourself, to check in with yourself, the solitude sojourn is definitely a time for logging off. No computer, no phone, and no kind of distracting devices. As I said, I might listen to music that has no words, and I might even listen to a podcast or audiobook—but its content would challenge me to dig deeper into myself. Not take me away from myself or make me forget.

In case of emergencies, you've got your second, emergency-only cell phone that we already discussed in our talk on logging off. If you want to use the GPS function on your main phone, bring it and put it to use. But remember that going off-grid, not infiltrating your brain with (non-emergency) emails and text messages, and removing yourself from all the binging is a luxury. It's an empowering and invigorating choice that will ultimately make you more grounded and in touch with what matters—both during your hundred hours of solitude and beyond. I even create an automatic reply email that alerts anyone who emails me that I'm on a tech-free retreat and I'll get back to them later.

When I talk with friends about these solitude sojourns, the reaction I often get is, "Don't you feel lonely?" Or "Don't you miss your wife and family?" No, it's not like that at all. In our talks, we've discussed accepting yourself, liking yourself, and being comfortable in your own skin. If you like yourself, you won't mind your own company. More than that, you'll actually enjoy it. When you're comfortable with yourself, then you're happy being with yourself. You don't fear being alone. It's not punishment. In fact, it's a rarely experienced and delightful pleasure.

About missing your family and spouse, sure, you'll miss them. But, we're only talking four days here. Plus, remember the old saying—distance makes the heart grow fonder. When I come back from one of my little solitude sojourns, I can't wait to give Sharon a hug and a kiss.

To repeat, I'm not telling you to go off for six months and hang out at the bottom of a dry well. It's just a long weekend. In spending this time alone and away, you give yourself time and space to gain perspective. And part of that includes reflecting on, and being grateful for, the blessings in your life. So, this hopefully means you're going to appreciate your spouse, your family, and your friends even more when you return. You'll bring back an even greater love and appreciation for them. Heck, you might even decide to give someone a call and have a heart-to-heart during your solitude sojourn, which is a totally legitimate way to put that second cell phone to use. Yes, you want to be as tech-free as possible. But a phone call that creates greater connection is not a distraction, it's a coming together.

When you're alone, you don't have to worry about what other people might be thinking about you, what you're wearing, what you eat, what you drink, what you do, whether you're leaving the toilet seat up or down. It's a hundred hours of zero judgment. It's a time of no worrying. Of hanging out with your good friend, your-self—who, believe it or not—you probably rarely get to spend much one-on-one time with.

So what do you do with this carefree time? For me, I bring a sketchbook and my trusty and ever present Montblanc pen. I use the sketchbook to jot down any ideas that might come to mind, usually ideas about another talk I want to share with you. And I also use it as a time to review my power visions.

In our previous talk on power vision, we discussed making a list or a vision board to record the things you most want to manifest. Take your list or your vision board with you on this getaway. If you haven't put one together, what better time than when you're alone on this trip? It's an ideal time to update your vision board and/or list. What's come to pass? What goal has somewhat changed? What new power vision do you have? Again, it's an excellent time to work on your vision board, and overall, it's a great time to plan, daydream, set goals, and take stock of your life. Your thoughts, dreams, aspirations, where you are in life, where you want to go, where you've been.

Some people say, "You should never look back." I disagree. I think you should because that's how you learn. Not only that, but think about it, *Let's Talk* is about making good memories, leading an exciting life, an easier life, an exceptional life. And looking back and reliving your memories, noticing what went well and why, and also looking back at your mistakes and seeing how you can learn from them—that helps you to grow so that you can live that exciting, easier, and exceptional life.

I take books with me. I think that reading is much better when alone. It sinks in better, even if it's just a novel that you're reading for fun. If you have people around you and they start talking, obviously, it takes you away from the world that your imagination is taking you to when you're reading. If it's a nonfiction book, whatever you're trying to learn sinks in much better when you're alone. I love to read when I'm on these sojourns.

It's also a great time to come up with ideas. I don't recommend bringing a computer, use a notebook or sketchbook to record ideas instead. It's also a great time to do research on a project you may have. For example, I might bring books, magazines, and printed articles that touch on a topic for a future talk I'm considering. I spend time gathering info from these. See your hundred hours as a time to reflect, plan, and daydream, but also to relax.

Don't forget to be thankful. I keep saying that I doubt there will ever be a more important talk than the one we had on gratitude. The solitude sojourn is a great time to be thankful. It's also an excellent time for prayer, for seeking divine guidance. What better time to be truly one-on-one with God? I mean, it's just you and the Almighty at that point. It's a good time to get into deep prayer, and then sit still and listen, listen for that voice that comes to mind, God's voice. It's a truly uplifting experience, and one we'll discuss more in the next talk.

If you end up missing your spouse, as already mentioned, you can call. However, I have a better idea. Write a handwritten letter or postcard, and mail it. That's much more effective than calling. You can do both, certainly, but I always love to take pen to paper or buy postcards at the little town where I'm staying, and send an actual letter by mail to my loved ones or to whomever. I'll usually take enough paper and envelopes with me to send about eight or 10 cards. Whoever I'm thinking about, I send them a short little note. You don't have to send a novel. It can be a brief one-page note or postcard. As I said, that's more special than calling.

Summing up, as I started this talk mentioning Gabriel García Márquez and his book *A Hundred Years of Solitude*, let's close with a quote from that book: "The secret of a good old age is simply an honorable pact with solitude."

Until we talk again, stay happy and healthy, my friend.

**12**

## TAKEAWAYS:

• Two or three times a year, set aside
four days, away from work, family, and
technology, to check in with yourself,
gain perspective, daydream, and evaluate
your life.

• It's a luxury to be alone. It's a time of zero
judgment from anyone, including yourself.

• Take stock of all your blessings, so when
you return, you bring back an even greater
sense of appreciation for everyone and
everything in your life.

# Two Ears, One Mouth

*We have two ears and one mouth.*
*So, we should listen more than we say.*
—ZENO OF CITIUM

**I don't remember** having ever learned anything while I was talking. Every single thing I've ever learned in my life, I've learned by listening or reading. There are probably thousands of books on this topic of listening, and we're constantly told that we should be good listeners, yet still to this day, we haven't quite mastered this very important practice. The reality is that God did give us two ears and one mouth, so we should heed what He's trying to tell us. Let's talk.

When I consider the people I admire, a quality most of them share is that they're very good listeners. You can literally see them listening. You notice that they're thinking too, and only after they think, do they give a reply to the person they're talking to. Listening is an incredibly important skill, and good listening is an art. One that requires immense discipline. For many of us, we always want to get in edgewise what we feel is more important to say. Yet, if we would learn to listen more than we speak, we could have better conversations and forge deeper connections. Plus, there would be less misunderstandings in the world. To get you focused on effective listening, visit www.RiosTalks.com and download the Talk # 13: Two Ears, One Mouth track from the audio book for free.

Through effective listening, our problem-solving skills improve. I can tell you that the successes that I've had in courtrooms, and in life in general, I don't attribute to great oratory, to giving incredible speeches or closing arguments. The successes I've had are the result of being very disciplined in listening and then assessing the situation around me before I act or speak. You can tell that I'm hardly the quiet type because I do love to talk. Hence, the title of the book, *Let's Talk*.

I love to talk to people, but effective conversations and strong connections require the ability to understand what the other person is saying, which hinges on our ability to listen. "Understand" isn't even the right word. We listen not simply to understand, but to really think through the words the other person is saying. Only when we've really immersed ourselves in their words can we begin to conceive and deliver a well-thought-out response.

I teach at Stetson University College of Law, and I have a saying that I always share with my law students: "*Con calma y piensa.*" That means, "Take your time and think." The class that I teach is about courtroom trial skills, and I'm always telling students—like I tell my daughters, and actually my whole family, who at this point are always joking with me about the saying— *con calma y piensa.* Take your time and think. And the reason why I say this is because, especially in a courtroom setting, you can't just fly off the handle and shoot from the hip. You need to be cognizant of what's happening around you. You need to be listening to what's being said before you react or speak. That's true in life, beyond the courtroom, as well.

*Con calma y piensa*, take your time and think, should be an adage that you apply in your entire life. Actually, in the next book, one of our talks is going to be titled "*Con Calma y Piensa*," where I talk a bit more about this concept. When it comes to listening effectively, *con calma y piensa*, take your time and think, is extremely important because you don't want to be in a rush to start blabbering things back to the person you're in conversation with. First, you want to take your time to hear and think through what they're saying. This way you can get on the same page with them. You can really know and feel where they're coming from. This will not only make for a deeper conversation, but it will forge a stronger connection and help avoid division, inaccurate assumptions, and misunderstandings as well.

For a conversation to be effective, there are four components to keep in mind. First, you should look the other person (or people) in the eye. Looking someone in the eye allows you to concentrate on them and not get distracted, for example, by what might be on your phone, anyone else around you, how your hair looks, whatever. Good eye contact allows you the focus needed to set the stage for the second element. Element two, listen more than you speak. When you're having a conversation with somebody, especially if it's serious, listen more than you speak. The third element for a great conversation is that it should really be focused more on the other person. Don't make it all about you. The final element, number four, you must care.

Indeed, the utmost measure of a conversation's effectiveness is caring about the subject you're talking about, the situation, and/or the other person. Because if you don't care two licks about at least one of these aspects, then the conversation isn't going to be interesting to you, and you're not going to put in the time or effort for it to be effective.

It is important that you let the other person talk more than you do. As Stephen R. Covey said, "Most people do not listen with the intent to understand, they listen with the intent to reply." It's more important to understand what the other person is telling you, to listen to what they're saying, than for you to be in a hurry to put in your two cents worth. Again, I think that's the biggest problem most of us have, that we're always in a rush to start talking ourselves.

This happens quite a bit. You're in a conversation and you're still in mid-sentence, but the other person's already interrupting and starting to talk over you. I see politicians doing it all the time, and I'm always dismayed. A reporter is asking a question, the reporter hasn't even finished speaking, but the politician is already answering. That's dangerous and disrespectful because you're assuming that you know what the other person is going to say. Or you're assuming that you're smarter than them. Another possibility, especially with a politician, is they're cutting off the question to give the answer that they want to give, which doesn't necessarily address the complete question that was going to be asked.

I'm even a proponent of listening when you're in prayer. Father John Suhar was the rector at my church for many years. He's a good friend of mine. He taught me that prayer is not a one-way conversation. Effective prayer is when you pray, you say what you want to say to God, then you sit in silence and wait for God to answer. Father John taught me that if you allow your mind to be quiet enough, and you're in a place that's quiet and peaceful enough, you will hear God's reply. That's what some people call that "little voice," "intuition," or something that you hear in your head, but I'm not talking about mental illness or anything. I'm sure you understand what I mean. It's God simply answering you. So, being a good listener extends to prayer. It's a wonderful thing to do because, as Father John would always say, "God wants to have a conversation with you."

As I wrap up this talk, simply put in your mind that you need to be a good listener. Take your time and think, *con calm y piensa*, listen to the other person, think, and then speak. Really listen. Do it with your whole heart. Give it your all. As Ernest Hemingway advised, "When people talk, listen completely. Most people never listen."

Until we talk again, stay happy and healthy, my friend.

**13**

## TAKEAWAYS:

- Listening is an incredibly important skill, and good listening is an art that requires immense discipline.

- *Con calma y piensa*, take your time and think, should be an adage that you apply in your entire life.

- It's more important to understand what the other person is telling you, to listen to what they're trying to communicate, than to be in a hurry to reply.

# Kindness

*Three things in human life are important.*
*The first is to be kind,*
*the second is to be kind,*
*and the third is to be kind.*
—HENRY JAMES

**My friend,** this may be the second most important talk that we share in this book, after our talk on gratitude, for I truly believe that kindness is the second most important character trait that a person can have. Kindness can move the world, kindness can change the world, and kindness can heal the world. So, how can we show greater kindness to one another? Let's talk.

Showing kindness to others costs nothing, and yet it changes everything. It makes the world a better place. It makes humanity more human, and at the end of the day, in the difficult times we're living in now, kindness is the one and only thing that will allow the human race to move forward with love, hope, and caring, instead of the hate, division, and the constant bickering that unfortunately seems to be at the forefront of daily life.

My loudest and most ardent call to action in this book, of all the many things we've talked about, is for you to show gratitude and to be kind. Of all the talks we've had, gratitude and kindness exemplify an exceptional life. The other talks are about making your life exciting and easier, and definitely showing gratitude and being kind will do that too. But above all, it's these two qualities that will make you and your life exceptional. With gratitude as the cornerstone of your life's foundation, it is kindness that keeps the rest of the structure up.

I was mentioning that it doesn't cost anything to be kind to others, and it really doesn't. What we may not realize is that even though we may be having a really, really hard day, it may pale in comparison to the hard day—or hard life—that another person is having. It may pale in comparison to their situation. We may think that we have it difficult, but in reality, they have it much, much worse. What's that old adage? "I cried because I had no shoes until I saw the man who had no feet."

I want to share something very personal with you. A story about my own transformative brush with the miracle-making power of kindness. Amazingly, it's a story that I've never told anyone before. Not my wife, my sister, my parents, no one. Seeing as I've already bared my soul to you in this book, sharing this very personal story from my life is only in keeping.

This story takes place in Puerto Rico. As mentioned already in our power vision talk, I started the first mail-order pharmacy on the island. Initially, I achieved a lot of success with the business. The business was going great because through it, I could provide prescriptions for people at significantly lower prices than the brick-and-mortar pharmacies. Sure, I was an entrepreneur, and I started the business to make money, but I also wanted to help people, as I've tried to do throughout my life and to this day.

As you already know, I ended up getting a lot of pushback from the brick-and-mortar pharmacy owners who took it upon themselves to find any way, under-handed or not, to drive me and my business away. As already shared, they were willing to play dirty to succeed, and while I'm certainly a fighter, I wasn't willing to play that game. I realize that may sound naive because some business people see playing dirty as a cost of doing business. Not me.

If you read this book's dedication, you see that I mentioned that my father taught me to be righteous.

Ethical. Because of my unwillingness to bend, I ended up declaring bankruptcy.

I still remember the conference call with my attorney and my CPA. I was in my company office. It was a large building with high-tech facilities. My attorney flat out urged me, "Art, you have to declare bankruptcy."

Sure, we'd won all the victories in court, but since the insurance companies and the pharmacies were being underhanded and shady, they were coming out on top anyway. Essentially, we'd won many battles but lost the war. And it was no longer worth the fight.

Then they both asked me, "So, what's your call?"

At that point, I realized that I couldn't continue fighting. They were right. It was time to declare bankruptcy.

However, it went against every fiber in my body to declare failure because I had always been a hard worker and I'd always been successful. Plus, if I declared bankruptcy, it would also be a public failure because the controversies I had with all the groups were very public, in the news, and all that. So, I had to make a decision, a very difficult decision.

I was only 33 years old at this point, and I'd put everything I had in the business. I'm talking blood, sweat, and tears, as well as millions of dollars. And I was going to lose it all. Plus, I had recently married Sharon. Maria had been born. Alondra was on the way. So I was starting a family in the most dire of circumstances, knowing that I was about to lose everything.

Bottom line, that particular day was a bad one for me. It was a very difficult day. I ended up telling my attorney and CPA, "I'll declare bankruptcy."

Heartbroken, I left the office. Bereft. Totally torn up. And even though I'm a Hispanic macho guy, I was crying in my car. It had been quite a battle, and we'd had victories, but again, unfortunately, I lost the war.

In Puerto Rico, along the older roads, there are rustic little establishments called cafetínes. Cafetínes are like small bars, but again, very rustic. Not fancy at all. You go to one to have a drink, a little fried food, stuff like that. They're famous in Puerto Rico.

I drove for a little bit. Like I said, I was crying my eyes out. I knew when I got home, I'd have to tell Sharon the news. But I needed to spend some time alone first. So I drove to one of the little roadside cafetínes. I went in, sat down, and ordered a stiff drink. I probably asked for a little something to munch on as well. Maybe an empanada or an alcapurria. I was wallowing in my sorrows, but not openly, just sitting there quietly. There were a couple other gentlemen there. But they left me alone.

A little while later, a man came in, and he was obviously homeless. He had a leg that had open sores on it. One of his eyes was filled with cataracts. I figured he couldn't see out of that eye. Pretty derelict.

He entered and asked the bartender working the cafetín, "How much food can I get for 50 cents?" The bartender looked at him like he obviously wasn't too happy to have the homeless man there, but he wasn't mean about it.

The bartender replied to the derelict man, "I'll get you a little something, but wait outside."

I said, "Hang on. Let's give this man a meal."

And the bartender looked at me like it was a bad idea, but I insisted, "Set him up with a lunch." (Cafetínes often offer full meals.)

I turned to the derelict-looking man and asked, "Sir, what do you like to drink?"

And, bless us all, Puerto Rican, he replied, "I love rum."

I told the bartender, "Give him a bottle of rum also."

Between the meal and the bottle, we're talking $15 or $20, maybe.

I'm not telling you this story to praise myself. I'm telling you this story because seeing this man in such apparent need at this particular moment of utter heartbrokenness in my own life put everything into perspective. It was as if God sent that man to show me that it was okay. That, yes, there were going to be tough times ahead, but I couldn't lose faith.

That's the message that I got the moment I showed the man a little kindness. There I was, losing millions of dollars, which was probably the worst moment for me to spend $20 on a stranger. But what was $20 in light of the millions that I was about to lose? And yet when I did this, immediately, it was like a burden was lifted off my shoulders.

Next, the man told me, "*Que Dios te bendiga*," which means, "May God bless you." I swear, that was an angel telling me that. And to this day, I believe that man was put there for a reason. Maybe he was an angel, I don't know, but his words gave me strength at the very moment in my life when I was at the lowest.

I'm not trying to get New Age on you, but even now, looking back on it 20-odd years later, it had to happen. I had to fall in order to rise in a much better way. I had to fall in order to rise in a way that was meant to serve others and not to serve myself. Because at the end of the day, while entrepreneurs do great things, the aim of the entrepreneur is to serve themselves and to make a lot of money. I believe that my fall from grace had to happen in order for me to be lifted in grace.

From that day forth, I simply accepted what I had to face—bankruptcy, the public failure of my business. Absolute humiliation. I faced it with the most dignified and brave face I could put on. Now, when I look back on it, I thank God that it happened. But it was this encounter with the down-and-out man that changed everything for me. And maybe my small act of kindness to him was the only such act that he received that day, or that week, who knows.

You don't know how an act of kindness that you show somebody can change not just their day, but their life. I always think of the incredible novel *Les Misèrables* by Victor Hugo, how one act of kindness by a priest towards Jean Valjean, the hero in the book, changed Jean Valjean's life for the better and put him on a course to lead a life of righteousness. The message—start showing kindness today.

When we show kindness to others, we shouldn't be expecting anything in return. Kindness is all about giving, and it has nothing to do with getting. Even still, for me in that cafetín on that terrible, horrible, no good, very bad day 20-odd years ago, that's what ended up happening. Encountering that man and getting to supply him with something he so desperately needed raised me up, giving me the faith and perspective that I so terribly needed.

One of the things that I believe defines kindness is making others feel important. And one of my big pet peeves in life is speaking badly of other people. I'm a big proponent of—"If you don't have anything nice to say, don't say anything at all." If you want to start showing kindness, simply do not say anything negative about anyone.

Sure, if you're a manager and part of your job is discussing people's strengths and weaknesses, that's different. I'm talking about normal daily conversations—don't say anything at all rather than be petty and mean about someone. Because at the end of the day, your kindness will define your happiness in life. And your kindness, along with your gratitude, paves the way to an exceptional life.

Mother Teresa said, "Let no one ever come to you without leaving better and happier. Be the living expression of God's kindness. Kindness in your face, kindness in your eyes, and kindness in your smile." Few people in this world were kinder than Mother Teresa. Those words should really resonate with us.

I like to do a little studying about the topics of our talks. When I did some research about ways to show kindness, I was uplifted by all the different websites and articles about being kind. One article I really liked was

"99 Simple Ways to Show Kindness" written by Melissa Eisler of the Chopra Center (chopra.com) in October 2016. Don't worry, I'm not going to give you all 99, as you must read Melissa's article, but I'll share my 20 favorites, or my version thereof:

1. Buy a box of granola bars, potato chips, drinks, etc., and leave them in your car. When you're driving and you see someone who looks like they could use something to eat or drink, give them something. Even better, always carry some five- or ten-dollar bills and give those.

2. Write an email to the manager of a restaurant, grocery store, coffee shop, etc., that you go to and tell them how great one of their employees was, how helpful and friendly they were. Or better yet, if you're still there, tell the manager in person.

3. Buy lunch for a friend or coworker. Don't even let them know. Or, so they don't go out and buy it themselves, inform them, "Hey, I'm picking up lunch today."

4. The next time someone cuts you off in the street, don't get mad, just give them a friendly wave. Maybe they're having a tough day.

5. The next time you hear gossip, change that conversation toward praise about the person or situation that everybody else is trying to knock down.

6. Give someone the benefit of the doubt. For example, your kids have told you something and you're not buying it—give them the benefit of the doubt.

7. If you see a lemonade stand, stop and buy as much lemonade as you can. Commend the kids on what a great job they're doing, and pay them a little extra.

8. Another biggie of mine is to leave your server an extra big tip, especially if it looks like they're having a rough day. But no matter what, always over-tip.

9. Hold the door open for a mom with a stroller, or anyone for that matter, and let them go in first.

10. Offer your seat to somebody. If you're on a subway, train, bus, or for whatever reason, offer someone else your seat and let them be comfortable.

11. If you're on a street or at a park, and you see a little trash on the ground, pick it up.

12. When you're ordering food at a bar or counter, the first thing you should do is ask the person taking your order, "How's your day going?" Start the conversation with that, instead of going right into whatever you want to order.

13. Help the elderly, whether by helping them carry something, retrieve something, or in another way, help them.

14. Forgive someone for something they may have done to you in the past. When you forgive, you just feel better. After all, holding a grudge is like drinking poison and expecting somebody else to die.

15. Make eye contact. The world needs much more connection. It means a lot when you acknowledge someone by looking them in the eye.

16. Say thank you. (Gratitude—again!) Anytime someone does anything nice for you, say thank you warmly. Feel and show sincere gratitude.

17. Write a note to one of your old teachers or professors thanking them for something they did for you.

18. Offer to take a photo for somebody who is trying to get that perfect photo or selfie and is apparently having difficulty.

19. If someone looks lost, offer to give them directions.

20. Strike up a conversation with someone you don't particularly like. Now, this one's very difficult for me because I like everybody, but there are people out there that make it very difficult to be liked. But those are the people we should reach out to and strike up a conversation with. And things may just change for the better.

When I graduated from high school, our principal, Mr. Fred Buckman, in the final school assembly asked that we, the graduates, do one act of kindness for humanity once in our life. One. That's because Mr. Buckman knew the power in numbers, and that if every single one of the 500 young people in the auditorium that day would show an act of kindness to someone in the future, the world would be slightly better. I send out the same challenge to you, my friends and readers, but I'm going to up the ante a bit: let's each do one act of kindness for humanity and our world, at least once every day.

The ultimate goal of *Let's Talk* is to help you lead an exceptional life. Exceptionalism means that you do things that are very, very important and grand. Showing a simple act of kindness to another person is all you need to do to be exceptional. So let's get out there and be kind, more often and with more people—both those we know and total strangers—more than we ever have in the past. Let's be extra kind because the world will definitely be a better place. Plus, you'll be happier by showing kindness because in the words of author Roy T. Bennett, "You should treat everyone with politeness and kindness. Not because they are nice, but because you are."

Until we talk again, stay happy and healthy, my friend.

**14**

## TAKEAWAYS:

- Kindness is the one and only thing that will allow the human race to move forward.

- Kindness is all about giving and has nothing to do with getting.

- Showing a simple act of kindness to another person is all you need to do to be exceptional.

# Racism Ends Now

*If origin defines race,
then we are all Africans—
we are all black.*
—ABHIJIT NASKAR

**I hadn't planned** to end *Let's Talk, Book 1* on a somber note. However, the senseless murder of George Floyd made me change tact. And yet, upon further reflection, I realize that this talk isn't somber, it's edifying. Uplifting. This is the perfect talk to end *Book 1*, for it is a call to action, a call for you, and all of us, to change. As Gandhi said, "Be the change that you wish to see in the world." Let's talk.

The simple truth is that I despise racism. To me, racism is used as an excuse not to think. Racism is used as an excuse not to feel. Worst of all, racism is used as an excuse not to care.

The Lord works in mysterious ways indeed. I had prepared my outline for this chapter and was ready to work on it when my youngest daughter, Alondra, asked me to help her with something. She shared how all the protests that Mr. Floyd's murder sparked had moved her. She flat out told me, "Papa, enough is enough. Racism ends now."

Alondra then explained that she had written a letter addressing racism for everyone in our family and asked if I could proofread it for her. My friends, I'm afraid she outdid her old man, for I cannot express my outrage and loathing of racism better than Alondra did in her letter. So, I won't try. Instead, with her permission, I share her letter with you because—enough is enough, racism ends now.

Familia,

2020—This has been quite the year, and we're only halfway through it! On New Year's Eve, I thought this year would be filled with graduations, celebrations, and transitions. I would have never guessed that, instead, it would be filled with chaos, seclusion, and introspection.

Let's see. It started off with the death of one of basketball's greatest legends, Kobe Bryant.

Then we heard about a murderous pandemic outbreak that swept through China, made its way to Europe, and then finally reached our shores. As if COVID-19 weren't enough, hornets made their way to the USA as well. Great!

Then we learned that Ahmaud Arbery, who was out exercising, had been murdered by two white men who took it upon themselves to "protect the neighborhood." Ahmaud Arbery. A name I hadn't known. Then Breonna Taylor was murdered by a police raid gone bad. Breonna Taylor. Another name I hadn't known. Then George Floyd was needlessly murdered by a police officer over a counterfeit twenty-dollar bill. George Floyd. One more name I hadn't known.

And yet, over the past three weeks, I've come to learn these names all too well. I've seen posts on Instagram demanding justice for these victims. I've researched, I've read, and above all, I've learned. I've learned that there are infinite victims whose names I hadn't known, and whose names I will never get to know, because their lives were taken away from them because of their skin color.

I am now a high school graduate. I'm an adult. With what I've learned about the deadly racism that is, incredibly, still pervasive in the United States, I cannot continue to live in a bubble. I cannot keep making excuses for myself, to protect me from realizing the revoltingly racist society we live in. I cannot continue to look the other way. I won't remain silent because I'm "socially obligated" to stay neutral. I won't remain silent because "it doesn't concern me." I won't remain silent because enough is enough.

After George Floyd's murder and the ensuing civil unrest, I felt torn. What could I do? How could I fight? What can bring an end to this? I've learned about the great activists and leaders of history: Dr. Martin Luther King, Marsha P. Johnson, and Malala Yousafzai. These are the leaders who fought/fight, for those whose voices were/are stifled. They were/are the leaders that sparked the need for change.

Well, I'm not them. I'm not the face of a national movement, but I am a face that you all know. You are my family. And while I might not be able to incite change on a national level, I would like to get the ball rolling on a conversation that we, as a family, should have because, at the very least, in our family, racism ends now.

When I took standardized tests in school, I had to mark myself as "Hispanic." When I applied for college, I had to mark myself as "Hispanic." On my resume for auditions, I put my ethnicity as "Hispanic." We are a minority. Yes, we are. We deal with our own issues. Even though I was born a US citizen, I've been asked by multiple people how I got my green card. I've been asked if I "took a raft" to America. I've been told to add some "Latina spice" into my performances. Yes, we face ignorant comments and microaggressions as well, but we—our family—pass off as white. Our skin is light. Our family is blessed with so many privileges, and one of those is simply that our skin is light.

There is racism toward Hispanics. But, as white Hispanics, we cannot begin to comprehend the unjust treatment that dark-skinned Hispanics and all Americans of color go through. Familia, we need to realize this, we need to change our mentality because, at the very least, in our family, racism ends now.

We, Latinos, are just as guilty of making racist remarks as any white person in America. Latinos are racists. This isn't a jab at Latinos because every ethnic group is capable of being racist. But, with that said, how many times have you heard a Latino refer to African-American hair in a negative light: "*Por lo menos, tu no tienes el pelo como esa negrita[1]*"? How many times have you heard a fellow Latino criticize biracial relationships: "*Tenemos que mejorar la raza[2]*"? Doesn't it seem odd that instead of calling someone by their name, many Latinos often say, "*El negrito,[3]*" for example?

I've memorized the common responses that I've heard when I've questioned someone for making ignorant remarks like those:

"*Es solamente entre la familia, yo no digo eso en frente de otras personas.[4]*"

"*Es un chiste.[5]*"

"*Bueno, es la verdad.[6]*"

Perhaps it's true. Maybe we do need to "*mejorar la raza.[7]*" But to do that, we need to better ourselves! We need to fight the racism we witness in the Hispanic community, at our social gatherings, and in our own homes. How? We talk. We learn. We think.

Papa always tells me, "*Con calma y piensa.*" Let's follow his credo. Think before you say something racist. Does it need to be said? Does it help at all? And most importantly, would you say that same remark if someone of that race were present in the room?

I know, you must think, "Alondra, *por favor*. Have you turned into one of those sensitive activist gringas who takes everything so seriously?" Well, yes, I guess I have because it is 2020, and it's time we finally put an end to this. I don't care if I'm mocked or called "sensitive." I'm not sensitive, I'm furious.

I want change. And since my family is the most important thing in the world to me, I feel obligated to open this conversation with you, so that we can all fight the true pandemic plaguing America right now: racism. It's not enough to just not be racist—we must be anti-racist.

Call me. Text me. Email me if you want to talk more. I'll be glad to. But I hope we realize this is not a fight that only black people must fight. This is a fight that we must all fight. We must stand with them. This is history in the making, and our actions, no matter how small they may seem, will dictate the future, not only of this nation, but of the entire world. To quote my fellow Boricuan thespian, Lin Manuel Miranda, "History has its eye on you." Well, history has its eye on our entire family.

Will we look the other way, like weaklings and cowards, and allow racism to persist? Or, will we be strong and brave, and do anything we can to trounce racism? No one in this family is weak. No one in this family is a coward. We're all strong and brave. But we must change. We must all admit that racism is wrong, and we must do everything we can to stop it, especially in our own minds and hearts.

I didn't know Ahmaud Arbery. I didn't know Breonna Taylor. I didn't know George Floyd. But I grieve for them because they shouldn't have been killed. Enough is enough. We need to change our mentality because, at the very least, in our family, racism ends now.

With all my love,

Alondra

---

[1] "Por lo menos, tu no tienes el pelo como esa negrita" means "At least you don't have hair like that black woman."

[2] "Tenemos que mejorar la raza" means "We need to better our race."

[3] "El negrito" means "the black person."

[4] "Es solamente entre la familia, yo no digo eso en frente de otras personas" means "This is only between family. I'd never talk like this in front of other people."

[5] "Es todo un chiste" means "It's just a joke."

[6] "Bueno, es la verdad" means "Fine, but it's the truth."

[7] "Mejorar la raza" means "to better the race."

---

Alondra, if every 18-year-old in our beloved country adopts your call to action, racism will end now. Take comfort in Pope Francis' words: "Situations can change; people can change. Be the first to seek to bring good. Do not grow accustomed to evil, but defeat it with good."

Until we talk again, stay happy and healthy, my friend.

**15**

**TAKEAWAYS:**

- We need to better ourselves . . . fight racism
  . . . How? We talk. We learn. We think.

- Think before you say something racist.
  Does it need to be said? Does it help at all?

- It's not enough to just not be racist—we
  must be anti-racist!

# Let's Talk Again Soon

**We've come to the end** of *Let's Talk, Book 1*. I pray you've enjoyed reading it as much as I loved writing it for you. I hope that you incorporate some of these ideas into your life, and that by doing so, your life will be undeniably exciting, easier, and exceptional.

I'm already hard at work on *Book 2*, so we'll have plenty more to talk about. Topics include saving and splurging, loving marriage, accepting imperfection, playing it by ear, small home/big trimmings, being HIP, competence, chilling out, sibling sabbaticals, and more.

In the meantime, please visit the website, RiosTalks. com, to continue the conversation. I've included some free gifts for you there as a thank-you for reading this book and for spending time with me. There's also a lot more content on the site that you might enjoy as well. And please send me an email, Art@RiosTalks.com, as I'd love to hear what you have to say about our talks. Thank you again for supporting my dream.

Until we talk again, stay happy and healthy, my friend.

# Acknowledgments

Writing a book is certainly not easy, and it does take a village. *Let's Talk, Book 1* came to be thanks to the help and unswerving support of some truly incredible individuals, whom I must thank.

First, ***danke schoen*** to my editor, the brilliant Nancy Pile. Nancy took my thoughts and made them readable. Nancy has always been supportive, even when being stern in her suggestions. Without her, this book would not have been possible. Nancy, I have tried so hard to find the words to show you how infinitely grateful I am for all your help. But, every time I try, I fall short, because I cannot describe my gratitude in a way that does it justice. God blessed me when He put you in my path. Just know that if you ever need a kidney, I'm your man. You are my Obi-Wan.

Next, I want to thank Jenny Hamby, my marketing guru. From the start, Jenny took me by the hand and has shown me many ways to get my message out. Her zeal for the project has been steadfast, and she made me believe I could walk with the giants of the trade. My message will spread, thanks to her genius. Jenny, you're my Yoda!

Thank you, Kathi Dunn and Hobie Hobart, for bringing color and imagery to the book and focus to the entire project. I also owe a lot to everyone at Self-Publishing School, as their guidance got the book into your hands faster, so you can make your lives exciting, easier, and exceptional that much more quickly.

And speaking of schools, I can't forget to thank every single person in any way, shape, or form associated with my alma mater, Stetson Law, as you are all my beloved and extended family.

I want to thank everyone at the Rios Immigration Law Firm. Kate, thank you for keeping my calendar organized, no matter how much I asked you to shuffle it around, and for your infectious smile and spirit. Vanessa, you're my left and right hand, and at times, a multi-handed goddess. Venus, if you hadn't kept the coffee flowing, I wouldn't have made it through the long days. Orly, your great humor and organization have kept me on track. You have all made practicing law easier, so I can have more time for *Let's Talk*. I owe a special thank you to Libby Even and Sergio Fernandez, as they were my initial proofreaders and critics. Sergio, you're the

Robin to my Batman, and you definitely make my life easier. Libby, your ceaseless and unbridled enthusiasm for this book was intoxicating and inspiring!

Albeit I mentioned them in the dedication, I must thank my family again because they are my everything, and without them I'm nothing. Mami and Papi, I literally owe you the whole enchilada, for had it not been for a balmy night in Aruba, I wouldn't even be here. I have learned so much from you, you have been great role models, and a lot of the talks in this book have sprung from your never-ending love, nurturance, and inspiration. My grandest aim in life is to be a great father and loving husband, and if I succeed, it will have been because I learned it all from the both of you.

I mentioned my grandfather, Papote, before in the book. To him family was everything, as it is to me. I cannot mention each and every one of you, as this book would become an encyclopedia, but you know I love all of you in the Rios, Rivera, Suarez, Baez, Zavala, Mattei, Caban, Padilla, Gonzalez, Rondinelli, and Marques families. And in that vein, to my foremost partners in crime, David Nolla and Jose Micheo, I wish I could remember all the crazy crap we did!

Can I say enough about my daughters?! Maria Fernanda, rarely is a father inspired and educated by his daughter, and you've done both. You're my rock, you're the person I trust most in this world, and your poise and pragmatism fill me with a tranquility I never thought I'd have. Alondra, you are my muse, little one. My love for you knows no bounds, and I sit in awe of what you have accomplished and of your amazing feats yet to come. Girls, you're my grandest treasures.

To my sister, Myrni, I love you, kiddo. My life is exciting, easier, and exceptional, simply because you're on this planet. And I can't forget my soul sister, Darby Dickerson. Darby, you mean oodles to me, and your "move to the left" changed my life forever.

What is more, to my beloved bride, Sharon, you are the greatest blessing God has given me, and I cannot bear the thought of waking up without you by my side. The road ahead for us is beyond exciting, our lives will get easier, and if I'm in any way exceptional, it's because you're my wife. I love you.

Finally, to you, my reader and now dear friend. Thank you for giving me a chance. There is more to come. Together, we will make our lives exciting, easier, and exceptional every time we talk.

Until then, stay happy and healthy, my friend.

# About the Author

Art Rios writes books. No kidding! He also practices law, teaches at Stetson Law, and enjoys long lunches. But above all, he loves spending all his spare time with his family. Art admits that he's a better talker than writer, which is why he enjoys the webinars, gatherings, and retreats he offers to further discuss *Let's Talk* topics. Good luck getting him to shut up at these events! Art is currently working on the next book in the *Let's Talk* series and is constantly adding new content to his website, www.RiosTalks.com. Reach out to Art—Art@RiosTalks.com—as he'd love to hear from you and strike up a conversation.

# Gratitude in Practice:
# Bonus Materials!

Although I mentioned them in the book, please don't forget to go to the website to get your free gifts, my tokens of gratitude for your buying and reading my book. I am eternally grateful for your support.

Go to: RiosTalks.com/free

Made in the USA
Coppell, TX
11 November 2020

41162244R00095